Praise for
Troubleshooting
Your Prayer Life

Terri has gifted us with an incredible resource. There is probably no one reading this who has not at some point cried out, 'How long, oh God!' We have prayed, interceded, decreed angelic assistance, fasted . . . and yet answers seem elusive. **Troubleshooting Your Prayer Life** *is the handbook you will want at your fingertips. It is practical, relevant, spiritual, and yes, it is REAL. Embrace it, and then recommend it to everyone you know.*

— **Tim Sheets,** Author of *Angel Armies, Angel Armies on Assignment, and Planting the Heavens*

"*Why are my prayers not being answered?*" "*Why should I continue to believe in God's goodness?*" "*Prayer is such a mundane task, why should I keep praying?*" *My friend Terri Brown has done an exceptional job asking these hard questions that many of us have. Then, she brings answers through learned life experiences and solid scriptural insight. This book will empower all who desire to engage in a spiritual journey into a greater intimacy with the Holy Spirit resulting in a pure, on fire prayer life. Thank you, Terri. I know many lives will be empowered as they glean from this honest, pure, anointed teaching.*

— **Rebecca Greenwood,** Cofounder of *Christian Harvest International, Strategic Prayer Apostolic Network*

Unequivocally, **Troubleshooting Your Prayer Life** *is one of the best books I have ever read on prayer. That is from someone who has been acquiring books on prayer for forty-five years, including eighteen years as Pastor of Prayer and Intercession, tasked with teaching, equipping, and mentoring prayer. Each chapter identifies problems and hindrances* *in our prayer life. Then Terri offers real life stories, scripture, and keys of wisdom to get our prayer lives back on track. This is not a read-one-time book, but an ongoing resource for times when your prayer life and relationship with God get off track.*

— **Mary Jo Pierce,** Author of *Adventures in Prayer, Follow Me,* and *Let it Rise*

Experience is beneficial in many aspects of life. It is especially valuable in the area of intercessory prayer. The experience that has been gained by my friend Terri Brown through many years of working with the Lord in prophetic intercession is an invaluable treasure that she has so wonderfully shared in her new book **Troubleshooting Your Prayer Life**. *Whether you are just beginning in your intercessory prayer journey, or you have been actively involved in intercession for years, the wisdom shared within the pages of this book is a wealth of knowledge that needs to be in the library of every prayer warrior!*

— **Gina Gholston,** Author of *Awakening the Church to Awaken a Nation, Dreams of Awakening,* and *Carry On*

Once you read **Troubleshooting Your Prayer Life**, *you will discover you have a great book on prayer! Terri's years of practical and personal experiences give you hope, direction and encouragement to seek Father God more intimately. As she shares her life experiences and lessons learned, you will glean applications you can use to become more effective in prayer. This is a book you will want to read, re-read, and share with others.*

— **Dr. John M. Benefiel,** Author of *Binding the Strongman Over America and the Nations*

Foreword by Dutch Sheets

TROUBLESHOOTING
Your
Prayer
Life

Connecting with God Through
the Delays, Detours, and Dead Ends

Terri Brown

Published by hope*books
2217 Matthews Township Pkwy
Suite D302
Matthews, NC 28105
www.hopebooks.com

Printed in the United States of America by hope*books
hope*books is a division of hope*media

First paperback edition.
Paperback ISBN: 979-8-89185-027-9
Hardcover ISBN: 979-8-89185-028-6
eBook ISBN: 979-8-89185-029-3
Library of Congress Number: 2023950996

hope✳books
hopebooks.com

Because the world needs your hope filled
words now more than ever

To Jack

This dedication might be the hardest thing I have had to write, because how do I put in words how much I love and appreciate you? Thank you for believing in me and this book, for working so hard so I had time to write. When I wasn't sure, you were steadfast. When I couldn't pray, you prayed. You have been my greatest advocate, and you have never tried to hold me back! Your joy and laughter have sustained me, not just in the writing of this book, but in life.

Thank you for loving me so well!

Acknowledgments

Jesus, you are my all in all. None of this is possible without you.

Thank you to all those who have taught me to pray, prayed with me, and prayed for me. There are too many to name, but I am so grateful for each of you. As I write this, I am thinking of people from the last forty-five years who have influenced me and walked alongside me in my walk with the Lord, and I realize how incredibly blessed I have been.

To each of my children, Jacob, Aaron, Caleb, Sarah Katie, Luke, and Annie. I count being your mother as one of the greatest privileges of my life. I am so thankful for each of you.

To those who have sat at The Table, whether one time or for years, you have enriched our lives. You are a blessing.

Dutch and Ceci, thank you for your help and encouragement in the initial stages of this book and your generosity in writing the foreword. Dutch, I remember so clearly you teaching on prayer and then declaring, "Some of you in this room are going to need to write a book on prayer." The Holy Spirit settled on me, and this is my offering back to Him. Jack and I honor and appreciate you both.

Martha and Mary Jo, your words, encouragement and prayers were extremely significant.

To those at hope*books and the amazing inaugural cohort, you have helped this dream and assignment become a reality. Thank you. We bonded in the trenches, and I appreciate each of you and am excited to read your words.

Contents

Unanswered Prayer

Regular Maintenance For Your Prayer Life

Foreword

by **Dutch Sheets**

Having been the beneficiary of literally hundreds of prayers offered up by Terri Brown, I can attest to her qualifications for teaching on the subject of prayer. Terri is a mature, seasoned intercessor. Unlike many, she doesn't teach theory; Terri teaches what she lives, having learned to pray the way most true intercessors have—on the job. And I consider her to be one of the best.

For twenty plus years, my wife Ceci and I have looked to a small group of trusted intercessors for our personal prayer support. Hundreds, if not thousands, of people pray for us—and believe me, we appreciate every one of them—but life and logistics only allow for a limited number of truly personal relationships. This inner circle of praying friends has watched us succeed, fail, rejoice, and bleed. They know our strengths as well as our weaknesses, and we trust them with information we share with very few. When faced with either difficult challenges or wonderful opportunities, we know whom to call for prayer. Terri is one of those trusted intercessors.

Though this book will help you pray more effectively, it is not just another "how to" book. Many good books exist with that in mind, some inspirational, some devotional, and others instructional. But you won't find many like this one dealing with—and pardon my colloquial slang—"What To Do When It Ain't Workin'."

Too often, spiritual leaders offer cursory, shallow answers to portentous questions, doing a great disservice to those they lead. Confusion, disillusionment, and cynicism are frequent and inevitable results. The reason for this dereliction by leaders is usually not that they don't care; it is simply that they don't know the answer. At that point, the simplest solution is just to attribute the more difficult issues—like why our prayers aren't answered—to the fact that God's thoughts and ways are above ours, and we can never really understand Him. However appropriate for some of life's challenges, all too often this overused response is just a lack of willingness to search out God's ways in the Scriptures. American Christianity has, sadly enough, become a very shallow movement.

Then there are the Terri Browns—those who are willing to dig for truth, even when the digging is in hard, unfamiliar ground. Terri has always been vulnerable and daring enough to ask Holy Spirit questions even when she knows she may not like the answers. She is a Christ-minded leader who cares about the frustrated "It didn't work for me" brother or sister enough to do some deep mining for them, to quarry the soil of God's word and search His heart until true answers are found. Meaningful answers. Sometimes even "I'm willing to try this prayer thing again" answers.

You're holding in your hands an honest look at tough questions—no formulas here. Yet, the insights it contains are not complicated. You'll find this book to be readable, easily understood, and wonderfully applicable. A troubleshooting guide to unanswered prayer? You bet.

Now, start reading—and praying.

Introduction

Endless books, articles, and sermons teach us how to pray and how to get answers to our prayers. Many examples of answered prayers are given as encouragement, and we love reading these stories that encourage us in our faith. In contrast, there are very few with testimonies of "I prayed for ten years, and nothing happened," or "I was suffering, so I prayed for healing and deliverance, and I am still suffering." If we are truly honest with ourselves, these perspectives are a reality for many of us. Genuine, faithful people are living these lives. Some will say, "You are praying wrong," or "You must have sin in your heart." Is this always the case?

If we look at Abraham and Sarah, how long were they praying for a baby after God gave them the promise? Do you think they quit praying when Sarah got too old? Were they still praying after Hagar had Ishmael? The story in Genesis Chapters 12-17 spans twenty-five years between the giving of the promise and the fulfillment of that promise. When God told Abraham that his ninety-year-old wife was going to have a son, the Bible says, "Then Abraham fell on his face and laughed" (Genesis 17:17 NASB). I'm not sure Abraham was praying and doing "it" right.

Yes, God answers prayers, and yes, God heals. Yes, God delivers. But we must be careful about saying that if we just live right and pray right and raise our children right, we can insulate ourselves from suffering. There is a mysterious side to God that cannot be simplified into a formula.

Love God + Keep from sin + Pray using proper techniques + Keep your heart right as you pray = God answers your prayer and insulates you and your children from suffering.

Have you ever stopped to think about what our religious formulas have done to the barren, those with prodigals, the sick, and those with chronic pain?

I'm writing a book to help people pray more effectively. It is needed, but I know it is risky. Some people might not pick this book up, thinking all I will offer are religious codes. Others may come looking for formulas or try to make what I share into one. You see, there *are* things we can do to pray more effectively. But there is no guarantee that your prayer will be answered immediately. If someone tells you there are guarantees, run, don't walk, away from them.

Often, formulas are created when a genuine believer seeks the Lord over a specific situation in their own life and God shows them something. They pray. Victory. Yeah God! Out of a pure heart they want to help others, but they end up taking what God showed them to do in their specific situation and "formulizing" it.

> *There is a truth in prayer that works, but it is not a formula. It is a principle rooted in a relationship: seek the Lord for the answer to your problem; when you hear from God, pray and implement what he shows you. This is the simplicity of the gospel, and it is the truth, but it is not a guarantee.*

There is a truth in prayer that works, but it is not a formula. It is a principle rooted in a relationship: seek the Lord for the answer to your problem; when you hear from God, pray and implement what he shows you. This is the simplicity of the gospel, and it is the truth, but it is not a guarantee.

Prayer is the way we communicate with the Lord, and just like in any relationship, when communication breaks down, the relationship breaks down. There have been times when I just wanted my prayers answered. I wasn't concerned about how my heart was towards the Lord. If He had answered my prayers in those times, I wonder if I would have been able to overcome the bitterness, anger, grief, or other things that I have had to deal with in my life.

Writing only about our successes makes the chasm greater between the haves and the have nots. The victorious will read about another's victories and vow, "I can do that!" And they usually will. In contrast, those who are struggling will read about a person's victories and conclude there is no possible way this could ever happen for them. They may conclude they are doing something wrong, or there must be something they should be doing that they simply aren't equipped to do. Down goes the book into a pile of half-read books. Another disappointment. They may even attempt to walk in said victory for a while, but because of a lack in skill set or discouragement or a multitude of other reasons, victory eludes them.

> *Prayer is the way we communicate with the Lord, and just like in any relationship, when communication breaks down, the relationship breaks down*

When we share our failures and how we overcome them, we move from pedestal sitting to entering the game as an encouraging teammate. We see these failure sharers in many arenas, but rarely in the arena of prayer. Maybe it is too personal or too painful, or it feels a little like we are blaming God.

So why write a book on *Troubleshooting your Prayer Life*? Because in over forty years of walking with the Lord and praying, I have dealt with unanswered prayers. I have learned how to overcome some of the hindrances to unanswered prayer. At times, I have felt guilty for the eloquence of my public prayers while being bored with my private prayers, feeling like a fraud for not praying more. God has patiently taught me, I have learned from others, and I have stumbled over some principles myself that might help you pray more effectively.

Praying effectively is important, not because it guarantees answers, but because we can be confident that we have done our part. No shame or guilt can be piled on us in addition to the tough time we might be going through. We can rest in the love of God, knowing the Lord isn't waiting for us.

> Since we have this confidence, we can also have great boldness before him, for if we ask anything agreeable to his will, he will hear us. And if we know that he hears us in whatever we ask, we also know that we have obtained the requests we ask of him. (1 John 5:14-15 TPT)

Prayer

"For here is eternal truth: When that time comes you won't need to ask me for anything, but instead you will go directly to the Father and ask him for anything you desire and he will give it to you, because of your relationship with me" (John 16:23 TPT).

And how does God want us to pray? He wants us to have contact with Him. He wants us to dialogue as a child to a Father. God wants us to reason with Him as Abraham did. He wants us to speak face-to-face with Him as Moses did. God wants us to know Him. He wants us to engage with Him. He wants us to call Him Father.

This truth can be expressed by saying we must abide in Him. Jesus told His disciples: "If you abide in Me, and My words abide in you, ask whatever you wish, and it will be done for you." (John 15:7 NASB1995)

Abiding in Jesus means living *in* Him and *with* Him. **It is the relationship God wants**. If His children walk in close relationship with Him, then He will answer whatever they ask" (boldface emphasis added).[1]

"I want to live my life so close to him that he takes pleasure in my every prayer" (Psalm 27:4b TPT).

"Let joy be your continual feast. Make your life a prayer" (1 Thessalonians 5:16-17 TPT).

Knowing
What to Pray

Chapter 1
Broken Heart

I had a pretty good reputation for hearing the Lord, praying in agreement with what He was saying, and seeing my prayers answered. I want to think I was confident, not arrogant. I had prayed our family through some difficult times and was an intercessor for several worldwide ministries. But as one of my daughters reached adulthood, I faced an experience that challenged me like no other.

The saying goes, "Hindsight is 20/20." This is true in many areas, but especially in parenting. We walked through an immense trial with Katie. Katie is a beautiful, anointed, and talented young lady who walked closely with the Lord while living at home. She wasn't able to go to her first choice of colleges because of financial issues. There was some misunderstanding over this issue, and she ended up going to a small rural college in Kansas. She tried to find a church or campus ministry to no avail. Disappointment, discouragement, and loneliness led to some bad choices, and traumatic events. The traumatic events led to seeking safety and comfort. This led to a relationship with a controlling man.

Before we knew it, we were standing in the yard in front of her rented house, loading up her stuff to take her home, when a baby-faced police officer showed up. He abruptly declared, "I am not leaving until you leave." He continued, "She is nineteen; you can't take her home unless it is her choice to go with you." We drove off with such despair we could hardly find air to breathe. Over the next four years we received very little communication. At times we didn't know where she was. Other times, we would get glimpses from my niece, Kacie. She remembered working at Sonic in central Kansas with a guy with the same name as the guy Katie was dating. She friended him on Facebook and was able to get info about them without revealing that she was Katie's cousin.

When tragedy hits, there are fervent prayers from everyone involved. Hope is high that God will intervene quickly. This was true for us as well. We prayed, we cried, we prayed, we cried. Repeat. Our friends prayed. Our family prayed. There comes a point–sometimes in a few days, a week, or a month–when we realize that we must move forward, because others depend on us. We realized our younger children, who were fifteen and thirteen, needed us to engage with them without always focusing on what was missing. This is not moving on. We still must contend in prayer, still grieving, but trying to live a normal life. We had to learn to sustain ourselves in the Lord during the gap between our prayers and His answers.

How do you pray when your heart is breaking? Emotions like fear and anger can run rampant, or emotions can be completely cut off to the point that your heart feels lifeless and dead. How do we pray when loved ones are making uncharacteristic decisions and things look hopeless? First, let's acknowledge that it takes fortitude to believe our prayers can make a difference in our loved ones' lives when they haven't seemed to yet.

It takes tenacity to contend. It takes courage to hope again. We may need to process emotions in the midst of the battle, acknowledging our anger, fear, grief, or whatever we are feeling. It does no good to suppress emotions, nor is it advantageous to let emotions rule.

At times I felt led to pray, but I wasn't sure I could open the door to the pain I would feel when I would go there. When I was praying from that place of pain, I was not sure my prayers were effective. There was pain and sorrow, but where was the faith? In contrast, I am not sure it helped to pray from an emotionless place either. I prayed, but it felt robotic and heartless. It was easy to fall into a place of measuring whether my prayers were good enough. My focus wasn't on my good Father, but on my weak prayers. I felt like such a failure as a mother, felt the judgment of others (whether real or perceived), and felt like I had failed as an intercessor for my own children. As I write this, I'm confident Jesus received every prayer, but from the place of anguish, I felt my prayers were ineffective and another reminder of how I had failed. Because of all the processing I was going through, there was a great temptation to stand in the outer courts and call out shallow prayers to God.

Other times, I began to pray and was greeted by condemnation or should-haves. I should have done this or said that or been better at that. Looking back, I saw many ways I could have parented Katie better and nurtured her more effectively, but I also had to receive grace from the Lord. I did the best I could with what I knew, with the maturity and healing I had at the time.

It took me a long time to get through all the condemnation and conviction. Some of it was the enemy condemning me, trying to discourage me. I had to recognize it and then go to Romans 8:1, "*So now the case is closed.* There remains no accusing voice of condemnation against those who are joined in life-union with Jesus, the Anointed One" (TPT).

On the other hand, I had to own what I was being convicted of. I had to grieve over my sin, repent, and receive forgiveness. 1 John 1:9 states, "If we confess our sins, he is faithful and just and will forgive us our sins and purify us from all unrighteousness." The danger I faced was getting this switched as I processed much of this alone with the Lord. If we start listening to the enemy, we will try to repent of things the Lord isn't convicting us of or things He has already forgiven. On the other hand, we might resist repenting of things the Holy Spirit is convicting us of, thinking it is the enemy condemning us.

This is why it is important for us to be able to recognize the voice of the Father and resist the voice of the enemy. Here are some concepts that helped me to differentiate:

God's voice lines up with His character. He is a loving Father, not a harsh task-master.

- The Holy Spirit convicts us of specific sins, while the enemy pours out shame and condemnation on us. Many times, the enemy releases a general sense of despair.

- God's voice lines up with His character. He is a loving Father, not a harsh taskmaster. Although He corrects and the correction can feel difficult, His voice doesn't release hopelessness, condemnation, or shame.

- We can hear God's voice. Jesus said, "My sheep know my voice ..." (John 10:27 CEV).

- We can learn to recognize how we hear the Lord by praying with others. As I listened and prayed with others, they would often pray something I was thinking, or pray a verse that had come to my mind. This gave me confirmation that I was hearing the Lord.

Like the warning of a flight attendant, "Put the oxygen on yourself first and then assist the other person." We must bring our broken hearts to him. Let him comfort us and heal us as needed so we can help, comfort, and pray for others. He sees our faults, but He loves us and comes alongside us, carrying our burdens.

Getting the Lord's strategy in the battle is key to victory. Occasionally, a prophet or a friend would give us a prophetic word or encouragement that would resonate with us. We would find renewed hope to pray for Katie with new hope, strategy, and vigor. One time my husband, Jack, heard the Lord telling him to release forgiveness towards the controlling man involved with our daughter. Releasing forgiveness is important, as we want people to be free. This seemed to be a shifting point for us. Asking the Lord for specific verses to war with, so we know our prayers line up with His Word or the prophetic words given to us, helps us to pray with confidence.

When we know how much He loves us, we can be bold! We can contend! We had to learn to persevere in prayer while trying to move forward in life. We couldn't focus on what was missing, but we could be thankful in the process. We never dreamed it would be so long until we received a phone call from Katie with tears, apologies from her, apologies from us, forgiveness, joy, and restoration.

This was the beginning of rebuilding our relationship. Every relationship has a narrator. It's that voice only you can hear, and it tells you what is going on in every scenario. The voice can stir up trouble by condemning us and telling us that others are condemning us. It can fill in with distortion and lies when we aren't sure what the other person means or feels. As Christians, the Holy Spirit should be our narrator, but in many cases fear or shame or greed or jealousy can become our narrator. All of these negative voices are tools of the enemy. We need to silence every false narrator to pray effectively and rebuild relationships. Katie and I were struggling in our relationship. I felt like I had let her down, and I think she felt ashamed of some of her choices. The Lord showed me that shame was the narrator in our relationship. As I tried to rebuild our relationship, I would feel such shame. We had a difficult time communicating. When I realized shame was trying to narrate our relationship, I took authority in prayer and banished this false narrator out of our conversation and relationship. The relationship shifted to a more comfortable place as our communication improved.

Father God,

Search our hearts. We don't want our prayers to be tainted by our hurt and pain. We know in this life we will have difficult times and we also acknowledge that we need your help to process these difficulties. Help us to hear your Holy Spirit, and to know when to repent and when to stand firm against condemnation. Lord, we ask for a Spirit of wisdom and revelation to help us know how to intercede. Help us to persevere through the darkness until we see the answer to our prayers. In Jesus' Name, Amen.

Symptom	Potential Problem	Try this Solution
I can't seem to pray because my heart is hurting.	Either not praying, shallow prayers, or praying from a place of pain.	Seek healing for your pain and seek the Lord for a strategy of what to pray.

Chapter 2
The Snare of Certainty

Praying is not as simple as choosing a certain destination, entering it into our prayer GPS, and then listening for the voice telling us what lane to be in, where to turn, and when and where to re-route. Unfortunately, some of us have become certain of what we think God needs to do and tried entering our plan into our prayer GPS, hoping God would listen to the voice directing Him. We then put our prayer life on autopilot, praying the same thing over and over. If Abraham had done this, he would have killed Isaac and lost his destiny (see Genesis 22:1–14). Yes, he heard God correctly, but he kept listening. God could see Abraham was passing the test, so God provided a sacrifice.

Do we think we need to tell God what is going on and how He should fix it? Trust me, God knows what is going on. He is more aware of all the intricacies than we are. My husband likes to remind me of this when I am struggling to figure something out or relinquish something to the Lord. He'll say, "The Holy Spirit is pretty big!" I'm not saying I like it when he says it, but just between you and me, it helps.

Our walk with the Lord is more about our relationship with Him than praying "right." God is not looking for believers who are Stepford Wives[1] who are cheerfully obedient with plastic smiles and no real feelings. He is seeking followers who are obedient but loving. He doesn't want us praying with the right words, but hearts that are disengaged. He is looking for real, honest, communication with His children. He wants us to be loving and trusting, but to admit when we are scared... angry...or frustrated.

If you know someone who is going to teach you how to get all your prayers answered, a guaranteed way to raise godly children, or any other "sure" way in this walk, my recommendation is to be very wary. There is a mystery in this walk. His ways are higher (see Isaiah 55:9). We can seek to learn His ways, but sometimes it feels like one of those puzzles where a picture is shown taken from an unusual perspective (magnified or from an odd angle). The goal is to name what you are looking at, but when the perspective is distorted, it is very difficult to decipher what it is. Much of our prayer life includes navigating our lives or helping those we love to navigate theirs. If we are not careful, we can pray from a distorted perspective. Expecting everything to follow a formula is definitely a common distorted perspective that believers can fall victim to.

It is important to remember His ways are different. To live, you die; to receive, you give. Those are just two common examples. We can read those statements in black and white and yet we still don't fully grasp these truths. The more we know the Lord and His ways, the more we realize how much we *don't* understand about His ways. I am very cautious around people who have stepped into the snare of certainty and have this life all figured out.

The more we trust God, the more we are able to yield our plans to His. We are very limited in our ability to see the big picture without His perspective. We may know where He wants to take us, at least in a general sense, but we may not know the methods or strategy. For example, I heard a pastor tell the story of praying with his wife, "Lord, align us with your destiny for our lives." Within a month, they were kicked out of their denomination. Not exactly what they were expecting! It took them a while to see this was an answer to their prayer. It seemed like a safe enough prayer for this couple to pray, but there are many ways to shift someone into the right alignment and not all of them feel like the moving forward or promotion we are seeking.

If in our minds and prayer life we are certain about the path that would be good for God to take, we may be hindering God from helping us move forward. Maybe you've experienced this situation before, but in settings like altar ministry, there are instances where people approach you not to request prayer but to instruct you on what to pray on their behalf. For example, "Pray God sends me a husband." I can totally relate to someone wanting a husband, but when we tell people how to pray, we limit them, and therefore we limit God. The person coming to the altar misses the opportunity for others to bring depth, breadth, or revelation to the desires of their heart.

Jesus wants us to spend time with Him, crying out, asking Him how to pray. When we listen while praying, it protects us from taking Scripture out of context and killing our Isaac.

Because by nature I am pretty resilient, the Lord had to get me to stop relying on myself. I come from a very long line of self-reliant people. My grandmother and grandfather's first home together during the Great Depression was a chicken coop that she cleaned out before they moved in. My first ancestor to arrive in this nation came over with the Dutch West Indies Company. Her family owned the land from Maiden Street to Wall Street across the tip of Manhattan Island. At a time when women were not usually allowed to chart their own course, she went to court to fight for who her guardian would be after her first husband was killed. She didn't like who the leaders had chosen. She also may have been the first person to be deported off this land after she called the fire chief a chimney sweep on her wedding day. She was deported for "tongue-wagging." She was sent back to The Netherlands and then brought back to America after her husband fought for her return.

I can so relate to this tongue-wagging ancestor, prone to say too much and certain of what needs to happen. It is a great heritage in some ways, but also a heritage that needs to be overcome because God needs us to yield and be reliant on Him. There is an assurance that comes with faith, but certainty flows from our soul: that is our mind, will, and emotions, and it is from a self-willed place, because we like our plan of how we think God should work.

God loves our passion and our pluck, but not from a place of self will.

We must believe that God desires to guide us daily. He is not a God who creates us and then pulls back and lets everything just play out. He is willing to give us daily divine guidance. He guides not only "big" leaders, but all of us. Remember Gideon (see Judges 6–8); he was the least member of the least tribe, and he wasn't sure God would speak to him. He put out fleece after fleece after fleece to confirm that God had spoken to him.

It is important to know how God speaks to us personally so we can recognize His voice. Dallas Willard was instrumental in helping me recognize God's voice.

> The question then is, 'What are the factors of God's voice that enable us to recognize it as his?' Also, in this case there is a distinctive quality with which we can become familiar—but it is not strictly the quality of sound as it would be with a human voice ... The voice of God will usually (though not always) take the form of certain thoughts or perceptions that enter our minds. The quality of God's voice is more a matter of the *weight* or impact an impression makes on our consciousness. A certain steady and calm force with which communications from God impact our soul, our innermost

being, incline us toward assent and even toward active compliance.[2]

Willard states that God's voice carries weight. I can remember times of debating back and forth in my mind about a thought or plan, and then something is dropped into my spirit that settles the argument. The idea is dropped in with weight. It is God's voice, His idea or plan, that trumps all other thoughts or plans.

Certainty is being sure we know exactly what and how to pray; faith is being confident in Jesus, His love for me, and His desire to guide and direct me in my life and prayers.

Maybe we can open our prayers with, "We love you Jesus, we trust you Jesus, show us how to pray in this specific situation." Once you hear Him, pray in faith. Until that time, pray in faith. Pray what you know to be God's will. For example, we can pray, "God strengthen their inner man, encourage their hearts. Help them to be steadfast. Let their body function the way you created it to function. Help me to walk in love."

I love it when God gives me a clear prayer strategy or when the Lord shows me a specific verse to pray. In the meantime, I pray what the Word of God shows me to be His will for all of us. As we yield to the Lord, our prayers become less about what we are certain God should do and more about finding His heart and then getting into agreement with what He shows us.

As we yield to the Lord, our prayers become less about what we are certain God should do and more about finding His heart.

One caveat about praying like this: there is no guarantee everything will turn out the way we prayed. We can be assured that we prayed in obedience. Often, another person is involved in what we pray about. God doesn't desire for us to be robots. He won't control another person's will to answer our prayers. Our goal is to faithfully pray until their hearts align with His.

Father God,

Thank you for wanting to communicate with me. Forgive me for any time I made our relationship plastic or about formulas. I want to be honest with you and with my feelings, but I don't want to be controlled by my feelings. Lord, I believe that you care about the big things in my life and the little things as well. I desire to hear your voice and pray in agreement with your will concerning what is on my heart. I break any vow I have made where I declared I could not hear you. Your word says your sheep know your voice (John 10:27) and I am your sheep, so I can hear your voice. I choose to release formulas and certainty and embrace this marvelous and sometimes mysterious relationship with you. In Jesus' Name, Amen.

Symptom	Potential Problem	Try this Solution
I am certain I know what God wants to do or I know what would be best, but my prayer isn't being answered.	The snare of certainty.	Admit you don't have the solution to the problems, but God does.

Chapter 3
I Have a Great Idea!

"Lord, we need you to heal Janie and George's marriage. Lord, could you give them raises so that they don't fight over money? Or Lord, you could give George a mentor who knows how to be a good husband? Or Lord, can you cause Janie to be more patient and content? Or Lord, I know it is stressful to have rambunctious boys that are two and four. You could have them be better sleepers. Help them to fall asleep by 7:30 pm and then Janie and George could have their evenings together. Lord, they really need to learn how you desire to have a marriage function. We pray for their pastor that he would do a sermon series on marriage, or maybe Janie and George could go on a marriage retreat. Lord, if you desire to send them on a marriage retreat, would you provide the babysitters and have them not ask me? Thank you, Lord!"

Wow! Have you heard people pray for all their good solutions? I have heard myself pray like this! I admit they are sometimes clever ideas, but they are *my* clever ideas, not God's. It can be discouraging to think we need to come up with the solution so we can tell God how to fix the problem.

It is easy to quit praying when we have this mindset of prayer as problem solving because we may not see a way for God to fix the problem. We want to avoid praying all the ideas we can see from this earthly perspective. I call this horizontal praying. Not only can this be discouraging, it limits our prayers to our good ideas.

Years ago, a group of about twelve of us gathered in a circle to worship and pray. One gal, in her desperation to see a situation remedied, named off all the ways she could see God fixing the problem. She named five or six different solutions that she thought of. As she paused for a moment, I heard one of the men mutter under his breath, "Do you have any other great plans to share with God?" His comment shocked us, and I'm not saying it was kind, but what he said was true.

When we pray horizontally, we pray from what we know or can see, not from what God is speaking to us or revealing to us from His Word. When we, in our rational or creative mind, feel the need to share our own solutions with God, we fall into praying horizontally. We stay on the same plane as our problem. Man's problem. Man's solution.

What if instead, we go higher and get the Lord's insight, seeking Him for the solution?

The passage of scripture where the disciples asked Jesus to teach them to pray always mystified me. He taught them what we call the Lord's Prayer, and then He goes right into the passage below:

> Then Jesus gave this illustration: "Imagine what would happen if you were to go to one of your friends in the middle of the night, pound on his door, and shout, 'Please! Do you have some food you can spare? A friend just arrived at my house unexpectedly and I have nothing to serve him.' But your friend says, 'Why are you bothering me? The door's locked and my family and I are all in bed. Do you expect me to get up and give you our food?' I tell you—because of your shameless persistence, even though it's the middle of

the night, your friend will get up out of his bed and give you all that you need. So, it is with your prayers. (Luke 11:5–9 TPT)

Surely, He is teaching the importance of persistence in our prayers, but there is another key lesson that many times is overlooked.

Have you ever had a friend come to you "on their journey" with something challenging going on in their lives and you have no idea how to pray for them? You have no bread to give them. Do you find yourself talking, advising, and counseling with them instead of praying? Do you just pray a generic, "Lord, your will be done," or do you pray some good suggestions of how God could solve their dilemma? It is easy to forget there is someone who always has bread. Like the man in the parable, we can persistently ask Him to give us some fresh bread for our friend on their journey. Remember this passage is part of Jesus' answer to the disciples' request to teach us how to pray.

God the Father always has bread. His thoughts are higher, His ways are higher (see Isaiah. 55:8–9). He sees things from a unique perspective, an eternal perspective. His heart is always pure and full of love. One key to knowing what to pray is acknowledging that we bring nothing to the table without God giving us something to bring. We can then come into agreement with what He is showing us.

> *One key to knowing what to pray is acknowledging that we bring nothing to the table without God giving us something to bring.*

Some of us were taught to pray as if we were writing a wish list to Santa. "I want this" or "I need this." Prayer is connecting with the Father, us listening to Him and Him listening to us. For some of us, the first step is to realize God is speaking to us. John 10:27 (NKJV) states, "My sheep hear My voice." Some versions use the word *listen* instead of *hear*. I love the idea that we hear *and* listen.

I like to listen to audiobooks through headphones as I am doing paperwork or housework. My husband will come in and start talking without seeing the wires coming out of my ears. He is speaking, but I am not positioned to listen or hear him. The same is true in our prayer time with the Lord. I sometimes have to do a brain dump, where I make a list of all that is on my mind, good things, bad things, tasks, and concerns. I list it all. Then, from a place of stillness, I listen for guidance from the Lord. He may give me an impression or picture or remind me of a Bible verse. On the other hand, He still may not speak to me about a specific issue, but at least I know I have done my part to be still and listen. I may have to keep coming back about a concern, but He hears me knocking with faith, knowing He has the answer.

Praying from God's perspective also helps protect us from praying prayers we shouldn't be praying. When our hearts are hurting, we sometimes forget the holiness of God and His love, even for those we are angry with or those who have sinned. Praying from the horizontal plane is especially dangerous when praying for those we love who have been victimized in some way. This is the time to be especially careful about how we pray. Let me assure you, the sooner I can get to the place of acknowledging I have no bread and going to the One who does, the sooner I can get in agreement with the Lord, and the sooner my prayers can become effective. I need to get His perspective and His strategies on a person or situation to move us forward. We can get so offended and hurt or jaded that when we pray, a Holy God could never answer our prayers because we are praying vindictively, selfishly, or with shortsightedness. It is God's grace that keeps Him from answering some of our prayers! We need to acknowledge we have no bread and ask Him, "How should we pray?"

Father God,

Show us how to pray. We ask for a spirit of wisdom and revelation over each situation on our hearts. We need to move from the practical to the supernatural.

I don't just want to pray for a solution that I can think of, but I want to tap into the supernatural. Lord, highlight Scriptures that I can pray for my friends and family. I want to agree with You. I choose to come up and get your perspective instead of trying to drag you down to mine. Release me from mindsets and limitations that keep me operating in a religious realm instead of a supernatural one. In Jesus' Name, Amen.

Symptom	Potential Problem	Try this Solution
I don't know what to pray. I have no idea how God can fix this problem.	Using my good ideas versus revelation.	Choose to not look for solutions horizontally, but seek revelation from the Lord.

Chapter 4
What Will Be, Will Be

I remember watching *The Doris Day Show* as a young girl. I would sing along with the theme song, "Que Sera Sera."[1] It is a fun and beautiful song that shows we can't control the future in our lives. It may help us overcome anxiety, but it is not good theology when it comes to prayer. It is fatalism; whatever happens, happens.

I wonder if much of the prayerlessness of today's church is linked with this "theology" of what will be, will be, so it really doesn't matter what or if I pray.

Throughout the word of God, He tells us to pray. I must believe if He is telling us to do something, it is because it serves a purpose, probably multiple purposes. For example:

- Prayer helps us develop a relationship with the One who hears our prayers.
- Prayer gives us a way to exercise our faith, which is pleasing to Him.
- Prayer gives us the opportunity to co-labor with Him.
- Prayer gives us an avenue to grow in our faith when we see prayers answered.

- Prayer can help us move from wanting our will to be done to seeing His will and wanting it to be done.

Many believe the only purposes of prayer are comfort, transformation, and developing a closer relationship with Jesus. In other words, there is no outflow.

Although I agree that prayer changes us, I also know that the Lord wants us to exercise the authority He has given us to affect change in this world. When the disciples marveled over the withering of a fig tree, Jesus replied, "Listen to the truth. If you do not doubt God's power and speak out of faith's fullness, you can also speak to a tree and it will wither away. Even more than that, you could say to this mountain, 'Be lifted up and be thrown into the sea' and it will be done. Everything you pray for with the fullness of faith you will receive!" (Matthew 21:21–22, TPT). He didn't say our frame of mind toward the mountain would change; He said the mountain would move. Prayer can make real tangible changes.

2 Chronicles 7:14–15, is an example of God waiting for our prayers and action before He acts: "Then if my people who are called by my name will humble themselves and pray and seek my face and turn from their wicked ways, I will hear from heaven and will forgive their sins and restore their land. My eyes will be open and my ears attentive to every prayer made in this place" (NLT). He is waiting for us, His people, to humble ourselves, pray, seek His face, and turn from our wicked ways. He wants to forgive and restore, but He is waiting on us.

Prayer can make a tremendous difference. It is not just a religious activity for our improved peace and karma.

Many passages in the Bible state that God calls us to prayer and responds to our prayers. In Numbers 14, the people would not respond with faith to the good report of Caleb and Joshua about the Promised Land and instead rebelled and believed the bad report. God declares to Moses in verse 11, "How long will these people treat me with contempt? How long will they refuse to believe in me, in spite of all the miraculous signs I have performed among them? I will strike them down with a plague and destroy them, but I will make you into a nation greater and stronger than they." Moses immediately went into prayer, praying not from a place of concern for himself, or even the Israelites, but out of concern for God's reputation. The Lord replied in verse 20, "I have forgiven them as you asked." God states He did something because Moses asked.

In Deuteronomy 9:19, Moses states, "But again the Lord listened to me." One more example is in 2 Samuel 24:17–25 when David cried out and made offerings on behalf of the people. Verse 25 explains, "Then the Lord answered his prayer in behalf of the land, and the plague on Israel was stopped."

> *Don't believe the lie of the enemy that your little prayers don't matter. They do, in a profound way!*

If you are thinking, "God is forgiving and kind, and He would have relented even if no one prayed," consider Ezekiel 22. The Lord speaks through the prophet Ezekiel, pointing out all the ways the Israelites displeased the Lord. It is a convicting list, not just to the Israelites, but even to the modern American church. Then He states in verses 30–31, "I looked for someone among them who would build up the wall and stand before me in the gap on behalf of the land, so I would not have to destroy it, but I found no one. So I will pour out my wrath on them and consume them with my fiery anger, bringing down on their own heads all they have done, declares the Sovereign Lord." It is sobering to me to note He was looking for one, not a big prayer group or a certain percentage of pastors, just one!

God not only wants us to pray, but He also hears our prayers. Our prayers can affect our own lives, the lives of our families, our city, state, nation, and the nations. Don't believe the lie of the enemy that your little prayers don't matter. They do, in a profound way! "The prayer of a righteous man is powerful and effective" (James 5:16b).

When you struggle with the idea that your prayers make a difference, try the following:

- Study and meditate on the Bible, looking for places where God answered prayer.

- Pray specific prayers that God can answer, and you can see the answer so that your faith may grow. Keep a journal of answered prayers, both little and large.

- Read books by people of faith who saw their prayers answered, like George Mueller, Heidi Baker, and others.

Praying with others and cooperating with the Lord in prayer can be extremely rewarding. We don't want to be passive and miss out on partnering with God to affect change around us. It is worth the effort to learn more about prayer and how to work alongside the Lord.

Father God,

Forgive me for believing wrongly about you, for believing you have already decided everything that will happen, and we are just robots in some predetermined game. We see in Scripture that you heard the prayers of ordinary people and responded to those prayers. I believe you desire to partner with me and hear my prayers. I come out of agreement with any vows I have made like, "God doesn't hear my prayers" or "God is just going to do what He wants anyway" or "We have sinned so much, we deserve judgment, it won't do any good to pray." I once again believe there is hope in these situations, and I choose to pray with hope and faith. In Jesus' Name, Amen.

Symptom	Potential Problem	Try this Solution
Not praying very much.	I believe prayer doesn't change anything except my internal life.	Repent of the theology God is going to do what He wants to do, and it doesn't matter what I do or what will be, will be.

Chapter 5
Forgotten Destiny

When I was a new believer, I would pray for salvation, blessing, or healing. (I had never heard of anyone being healed, so it was more about them getting to the right doctor and getting the right medicine.) Maybe a little more than that, but not much.

I had no understanding of destiny. There are many verses in the Bible that refer to our destiny.

My frame was not hidden from you when I was made in the secret place, when I was woven together in the depths of the earth. Your eyes saw my unformed body; all the days ordained for me were written in your book before one of them came to be.

How precious to me are your thoughts, God!
How vast is the sum of them! (Psalm 139:15-17).

All the stages of my life were spread out before you,
The days of my life all prepared
before I'd even lived one day (Psalm 139:16b MSG).

I know the plans I have for you," declares the Lord, "plans to prosper you and not to harm you, plans to give you hope and a future (Jeremiah 29:11).

For we are God's handiwork, created in Christ Jesus to do good works, which God prepared in advance for us to do (Ephesians 2:10).

We have become his poetry, a re-created people that will fulfill the destiny he has given each of us, for we are joined to Jesus, the Anointed One. Even before we were born, God planned in advance *our destiny* and the good works we would do *to fulfill it*! (Ephesians 2:10) TPT

God has a wonderful plan for our lives, and when we are praying for ourselves and others, we want to tap into His plan. We want to be praying prayers that cause us to move forward towards the good works that God has prepared for us to do (see Ephesians 2:10 above).

He gifts us with anointing so that we can carry out these God-given assignments, but many times we are unable to accomplish the good works that God has given us, because we don't have the character required for these tasks. It could be that we are lazy or dishonest. Maybe we walk in anger, pride, or lust. Even though we have the anointing and the opportunity, we may lack the character to walk out what God has called us to do. We want to pray prayers that call forth the character required to accomplish all God has prepared for us or for those we are praying for. We are not praying in a vacuum or praying pin the tail on the donkey.

We want to align with God's heart and purposes for the person, family, church, city, state, or nation we are praying for.

There are several ways to do this:

- Many prayers are generic to every destiny: "Lord, help them to walk in humility. Give them a love for your word." Every believer, no matter what their destiny, will benefit from walking in humility and loving His word.

- Some things are more specific to a person's calling: "Lord, give him a heart for the poor and downtrodden." "Lord, give her the boldness to be the evangelist you called her to be."

- Some prayers that are very specific. For example, we might pray these prayers for a person called to be a medical doctor and researcher: "Lord, I ask that you give Kevin a healing anointing as well as the discipline to study. We ask that you give him the overtaking blessing as he takes the MCAT. Even when he must guess on a question, let him guess correctly. Give Kevin creative ideas as he researches illnesses."

What if we don't know our destiny or the destiny of others?

First, acknowledge that we each have a destiny and it matters how we pray. When I was a young mother with two-year-old twin sons, I went to a class, led by a lady from my church, using the booklet *How to Pray for Your Children* by Quin Sherrer. (Quin has re-written the booklet into a book and I highly recommend it. It is still available on Amazon.)[1] Here I was, a young mom and a fairly new believer, with no idea what to pray for these two sweet, rambunctious boys. One of the first things the book taught was to ask the Lord to show you what to pray for your child. He knows their destiny and what they need more than we, as parents, do.

Within one week, I caught my son Jacob in two lies. I didn't hear God speak to me, He just allowed me to see something I had not seen before. So, I really prayed for Jacob to be honest, and we parented in a way that didn't tolerate lies. I don't think I ever caught him in a lie the rest of the years he lived in our home. He now is a research analyst that uses statistics and data to help create and change public policy. It would undermine his career if he were prone to lie and fabricate data. God knew what he needed. I just needed to tap into His knowledge about my son.

I didn't see the significance of this prayer for Jacob until much later. It was not like I saw the big plan for his life and intentionally did things to get him there. I simply asked the One who created him and held his destiny, "How should I pray?" We often don't see the answers or significance of our prayers for a long time, but that doesn't make them any less significant. Importantly, I am not praying my son does what I am certain he would be good at or hoping he would fulfill some self-led desire of mine, but that his life aligns with the destiny spoken of in Ephesians 2:10: "God planned in advance *our destiny* and the good works we would do *to fulfill it*"! (TPT)

We can also ask God to show us, in His word, verses that apply to a person's destiny. God may also use others to speak into our destinies. This person might hear, see, or dream something from the Lord on behalf of us or on behalf of a church or location. Many times, this will confirm what God was already showing us, but sometimes the word will be what I call a "shelf prophecy." This type of word gives us a glimpse of something in our future that is hard to believe right now, but also resonates with our spirit. It is not contrary to the Word or what He has been speaking; it is just hard to believe right now. So, I set it on a shelf and let the Lord bring it down when He is ready. I might dust it off from time to time (which is praying into it) but it is not my focus today.

We want to always test prophetic words. Do they align with *the* Word? Is it carrying the right spirit? (For example, if it feels condemning, that is not the Lord.) Does the person delivering seem to have pure motives and good character? "Do not stifle the Holy Spirit. Do not scoff at prophecies, but test everything that is said. Hold onto what is good" (1 Thessalonians 5:19–21, NLT).

About twenty-five years ago, Jack and I were pastoring in Missouri and had traveled to Colorado Springs for a conference. There were no Wednesday night activities at the conference, so we sought out a local church pastored by Dutch Sheets. We had read his excellent book, *Intercessory Prayer,* and we looked forward to hearing him speak. Unbeknownst to us, but not to God, we had a call to Colorado Springs. We went to this meeting, not knowing that it was part of what they were calling "City Church." That night, many churches gathered together to hear a prophet declare the destiny of the city. God had a divine appointment, so we, who were called to the city, could hear firsthand His purposes and plans for the city. It gave us insight and wisdom about how to pray, and it helps us pray for our region even to this day.

The church of Colorado Springs went through a difficult season because of scandals and division in the body of Christ. Some left, in what we call the "Texodus," and it was being said God had lifted His hand off this city.

In the spring of 2015, my husband and I gathered 12–15 key prophetic intercessors and leaders in the city. These were people we knew from many different churches in Colorado Springs who had prayed for the city in the past. We didn't know what they were doing now, but we wanted to get them together to listen to what they were hearing over the city.

As we gathered, there was a consensus that God was telling us that this was a "now" time for our city. Several felt this was like the time of Nehemiah rebuilding the wall, others saw the picture of the dry bones coming together in Ezekiel 37. We all agreed there are no expiration dates on destiny. We knew we had no righteous leg to stand on, but we did know God was a covenant keeping God. It wasn't because people in our city were doing all the right things, or because Colorado Springs was a bastion of unity and holiness, or because of anything we had done or could do, but because of the faithfulness of God. We knew the calling of the city and we held onto it by crying out to God and rehearsing back to Him what He had disclosed concerning Colorado Springs.

We all agreed there are no expiration dates on destiny.

When ministries started moving back to the city, one leader said, "I am not surprised that God still wants to use the city, but I am surprised by the shortness of the turnaround. I attribute the speed of the turnaround to the intercessors holding onto the destiny of the city."

If we had all agreed with what God desired to do in our city and then stepped into the mentality of "What will be, will be," like we discussed in the last chapter, I don't believe we would have seen the turnaround. We believed 2 Chronicles 7:14: "If my people, who are called by my name, will humble themselves and pray and seek my face and turn from their wicked ways, then I will hear from heaven, and I will forgive their sin and will heal their land." We humbled ourselves, prayed, sought His faces, and turned from our wicked ways. We prayed in agreement with what He showed us was His will.

I wish I could say our city is totally transformed; it is not. We have seen victories and setbacks and are once again in a season of applying 2 Chronicles 7:14. I remember someone saying once, "We don't lose unless we give up." We will look into this further in Chapter 18.

There are some key things for us to remember when praying for destiny to be fulfilled:

- Ask God to show you how to pray.
- Reread prophetic words given to yourself, others, cities, and nations. Declare them, pray into them.
- Be in settings where prophetic words are given.
- Ask God to show you His plans for you or others.
- Remember, God is not trying to keep it a secret, we please Him when we search it out.

Dear Lord,

I receive the truth that I have a destiny and those who I pray for do too. Help me to know how to pray for my family and those you have assigned me to pray for, so my prayers line up with their prophetic destiny. In Jesus' Name, Amen.

Symptom	Potential Problem	Try this Solution
I don't know what to pray.	Forgetting God has a destiny for people and places.	Ask God to show you the person's or place's destiny and pray in agreement with it.

Chapter 6
Say What?

He blurted this out without thinking, stunned as they all
were by what they were seeing (Mark 9:6 MSG).

For he did not [really] know what to say because they were
terrified [and stunned by the miraculous sight] (Mark 9:6
AMP).

This is one of my favorite verses in the Bible, because I can relate
to it so much! "He blurted this out without thinking." Oh, so
many times in my life I have done this.

In this passage, Peter, James, and John go up on a high mountain with Jesus. Jesus' appearance totally changes. His clothes become supernaturally dazzling white, and then Elijah and Moses appear and begin talking with Jesus. Maybe because he is shocked or
overwhelmed, Peter reacts by giving Jesus the great idea of building
a tabernacle. Wait, not just one, but three. Can you imagine seeing
this unfold?

When things occur out of our norm, like incredible miracles or
encounters with an all-powerful God, or even devastating news, we
too, can feel like Peter, spouting off whatever comes to mind in the
moment. In our nervousness we may feel uptight or skittish. It is ac-
ceptable to be shocked and unsure of what to say or do, but it might

be best to be still, pause, and then respond instead of immediately reacting in the moment.

When praying, there are times we don't know what to pray. We are concerned but clueless. This is a good place to be. We don't have to surrender our amazing ideas, because we don't have any! This is an appropriate time to worship and praise the Lord, or thank Him, or pray in tongues. Don't just say words to say words. There is nothing I know of that clears the Holy Spirit out of prayer meetings faster than someone praying words just to fill the quiet. (Just as a side note: Yes, the Holy Spirit does leave prayer meetings. If you have never noticed, trust me. I have experienced it many times, sometimes in the prayer meetings I was leading!) Jesus explained this in the Sermon on the Mount. "When you pray, don't babble on and on as the Gentiles do. They think their prayers are answered merely by repeating their words again and again" (Matthew 6:7 NLT).

Joyce Meyers, a well-known Bible teacher known for her practical wisdom, explains how God has taught her to pray:

> I believe God has instructed me to make my requests of Him with as few words as possible. As I follow this practice, I understand more and more why He has asked me to pray this way. I find if I can keep my requests simple and not confuse the issue by trying to come up with too many words, my prayers actually are more clear and powerful.

> We need to spend our energy releasing our faith, not repeating phrases over and over when they only serve to make our prayers long and involved.

> I am not advocating praying only for a short period of time, but I am suggesting that each prayer be simple, direct, to the point, and filled with faith.[1]

Along with Joyce Meyer's advice to keep it simple, our prayers can go deeper as we learn to be still, rest in Him and then respond.

Be still and know that I am God (Psalm 46:10a NKJV).

Surrender your anxiety. Be still and realize that I am God (Psalm 46:10a TPT).

This is what the Sovereign Lord, the Holy One of Israel, says: "Only in returning to me and resting in me will you be saved. In quietness and confidence is your strength" (Isaiah 30:15 NLT).

Don't be scared to just be quiet. It's okay to let a prayer meeting go silent. The problem with allowing silence is that usually the one person most uncomfortable with silence will try to fill the silence. What if we were quiet until the Lord filled the silence? It can happen, but we must train ourselves and others to be okay with silence.

What if we were quiet until the Lord filled the silence? It can happen

If one can't be quiet, there may be a need for practice. But if one is not able to quiet the mind, there may be a need for deliverance. There are whole books written on deliverance and how the Lord sets people free, so I won't go into the details, but let me share this picture in case the concept of deliverance is new to you. Imagine your brain is like a room with doors. When you believe in the Lord Jesus and are filled with the Holy Spirit, the Holy Spirit has an open door to access your thoughts. This is how God works to bring helpful verses to mind or reminds you of someone you haven't thought of in a while. We recognize it as the Lord's reminder when we reach out to that person, and it happens to be precisely when they truly needed a friend or some encouragement.

There is another door where the enemy tries to enter with thoughts that might discourage, harass, or tempt us. We can shut that door by saying, "In the name of Jesus, I will not receive this condemnation or whatever the enemy is trying to send my way." This is taking thoughts captive as described in 2 Corinthians 10:5: "We demolish arguments and every pretension that sets itself up against the knowledge of God, and we take captive every thought to make it obedient to Christ."

Sometimes we can give the enemy an open door to our minds. For example, we can do this by participating in sin without repentance, or believing lies about ourselves or God. Satan is a legalist, and if he has a legal right to harass, he takes advantage of the open door.

Deliverance helps us see where the legal right is, so we can shut the door and keep it shut with the help of the Holy Spirit. It entails asking forgiveness, and revealing lies and coming out of agreement with those lies. It involves taking back the legal authority the enemy has been using to harass us. In essence, we are shutting the door the enemy uses to send thoughts our way that hinder our walk with the Lord.

Often, once people receive deliverance, they are shocked at the silence in their minds. We are not talking about mental illness here, just the reality of the enemy trying to influence the believer with his many words.

Just to reiterate, when you don't know what to pray and you are tempted to just say words to say words, take the following steps:

- Don't be afraid to be still. "Be still and know that I am God" (Psalm 46:10), or as it says in the Passion Translation, "Surrender your anxiety! Be silent and stop your striving and you will see that I am God."

- Worship and exalt Him. "Lord, you are loving, kind, all-powerful, holy. 'You will keep in perfect peace all who trust in you, all whose thoughts are fixed on you!'" (see Isaiah 26:3, NLT).

- Thank Him. "Thank you, Lord, for sustaining me, for loving my children." Remember, "Be thankful in all circumstances, for this is God's will for you who belong to Christ Jesus" (1 Thessalonians 5:18 NLT).

- Pray in your spirit or in tongues. This takes us out of a place of trying to communicate with the Lord through our minds, where language is centered. We can communicate spirit to Spirit. "But you, *my* delightfully loved friends, constantly and progressively build yourselves up on the foundation of your most holy faith by praying every moment in the Spirit" (Jude 1:20 TPT).

Lord, we thank you for desiring to communicate with us, and we don't have to always know how to pray. We trust that we can be silent before you. You are not a stern father demanding for us to speak up. You are a patient Father. It is okay for us to just sit in your presence and sigh. Thank you for being a safe God. In Jesus' Name, Amen.

Symptom	Potential Problem	Try this Solution
I don't know what to pray.	Praying the first thing that comes to mind. Having a hard time being quiet with your mouth and in your mind.	Be still. Learn to respond in prayer instead of reacting.

Troubleshooting Guide
For
Knowing What to Pray

Symptom	Potential Problem	Try this Solution	Chapter
I can't pray because my heart is hurting.	Not praying, shallow praying, or praying from a place of pain.	Seek healing for your pain and seek the Lord for a strategy of what to pray.	1
I am certain I know what God wants to do or what would be best, but my prayer isn't being answered.	The snare of certainty.	Admit you don't have the solution to the problem, but God does.	2
I don't know what to pray. I don't know how God can fix this problem.	Using my good ideas versus seeking revelation.	Choose to not look for solutions horizontally, but seek revelation from the Lord.	3

Not praying very much.	I don't believe prayer changes anything except my internal life.	Repent of the theology God is going to do what He wants to do, and it doesn't matter what I do or what will be, will be.	4
I don't know what to pray.	Forgetting God has a destiny for people and places.	Ask the Lord to show you a person's or places destiny and pray in agreement with it.	5
I don't know what to pray.	Praying the first thing that comes to mind and having a hard time being quiet with your mouth and in your mind.	Be still. Learn to respond in prayer instead of reacting.	6

Knowing
How to Pray

Chapter 7
Quiet Please!

Distracted, over stimulated, confused, and overloaded with information. This describes the typical American with the technology of the twenty-first century. But does it also describe the typical Christian? Unfortunately, we probably would all agree that far too often it does. Most of us struggle to find the quiet we need to fellowship with the Lord.

There are many scriptures reminding us of the importance of being quiet.

- Now stand here quietly before the Lord as I remind you of all the great things the Lord has done for you and your ancestors (1 Samuel 12:7 NLT).
- I wait quietly before God, for my victory comes from him (Psalm 62:1 NLT).
- Let all that I am wait quietly before God, for my hope is in Him (Psalm 62.5 NLT).

Many of us try to hear and be intimate with the Lord with the television blaring or while scrolling through the internet, Facebook, Twitter, or email. This doesn't even count the distractions of the real people that we live with. We wonder why we feel disconnected and unheard. Could it be that something so simple as finding a quiet place can make a difference? Yes!

If David, who lived before radio, television, internet, smart phones, and dumb phones, needed to wait quietly before the Lord, what should we do amid the incessant demands of media and technology? Maybe you find your quiet in a special place in your house, in the car while driving to work, or in nature. We all are wired differently. Some can even find their quiet place surrounded by people at the busy local coffee shop. The key is that we are diligent in our efforts to find that place.

My friend Mary Jo Pierce is the author of three books on prayer, including *Adventures in Prayer,* in which she explains she has a prayer chair and a separate listening chair. She sits in one chair while praying or reading her Bible, but when she wants to listen, she moves to the other chair. What a great idea! Whether or not we have two physical chairs, we can all make that distinction of posturing ourselves to listen.

Some of us have heard the story of how Susanna Wesley, the mother of John and Charles Wesley, who were influential eighteenth century English religious leaders, would find her quiet place by putting her apron over her head while mothering eleven children. The children learned to respect their mother's time of praying.

We want to give more than casual glances towards the Lord.

God knows our situation. We don't need to be legalistic, but we want to give more than casual glances towards the Lord. As the Psalmist declares, "You're my place of quiet retreat; I wait for your word to renew me" (Psalm 119:114 MSG). Not only is there a place of quiet retreat, but it is also a place of renewal. There are so many times when I need to be renewed after pouring out to others. The temptation I face is that I think binge watching a favorite show or mindlessly perusing Facebook will renew me. Sometimes I feel a little rested after that, but I rarely feel renewed. Like David, I need to realize that God is my place of quiet retreat, and I need to wait for His Word to renew me.

Exhaustion is a status symbol in many Christian circles, but I don't believe it is God's plan for us. He wants to renew us. My favorite place of renewal is sitting next to a stream, drinking in the quiet, resting in His Word.

There can be an awkwardness to stillness. Some of us get very uncomfortable and fill the void with our words and actions. I remember being in a corporate worship gathering where the worship team went into a time of silence. We all stood there in silence. After several minutes, we heard a distant noise. It was pleasant but unusual, a different kind of sound. I could tell that those around us could hear it too, because we were glancing at each other with raised eyebrows and then over toward the sound. I believe it may have been angels beginning to sing. Unfortunately, those leading the meeting couldn't hear what we heard and shifted the meeting. What are we missing individually and corporately because we are uncomfortable being quiet?

Try being still before the Lord for five minutes. No worship music, no Bible reading, no praying in tongues, just quiet.

Did you try it?

Did your mind wander? Did you see things that needed to be done? Did you think about what you were going to fix for dinner? Or were you tempted to do something other than focus on Him and be still before Him? Did you make requests of the Lord or pray in tongues or anything else?

As I reread this, I tried the five minutes of silence. After struggling for a few minutes, I prayed, "In the name of Jesus, I take authority over any spirits of distraction trying to harass me. I plead the blood of Jesus over my mind. I declare I have the mind of Christ" (1 Corinthians 2:16). Spirits of distraction are the spirits whose job is to distract us, but in this case, it wasn't the issue because nothing changed. The distractions were within, not from the outside. I had to slow down and acknowledge what was distracting me. I wrote down items I needed to remember, the grocery list, and a reminder to write a note to a friend who I was concerned about. I prayed for the child I was concerned for until I felt some peace over the situation. I then turned my gaze back to the Lord and could be still in His presence. If not already in the presence of God, it takes discipline to get into the quiet place.

"Here's what I want you to do: Find a quiet, secluded place so you won't be tempted to role-play before God. Just be there as simply and honestly as you can manage. The focus will shift from you to God, and you will begin to sense his grace" (Matthew 6:6 MSG).

Dear Lord,

We acknowledge that quiet is significant in our relationship with You. As you say in Psalm 46:10, "Be still, and know that I am God." We choose to be still. We choose to be quiet before You. We choose to give You time and access to all of us, our mind, our thoughts, our emotions. Help us find that quiet place with You where we open ourselves up to You. We choose not to hide in busyness and noise. We yield to You, to Your ways, to Your voice. In Jesus' Name, Amen.

Symptom	Potential Problem	Try this Solution
I keep getting distracted when I am trying to pray.	Lack of quiet and too many distractions.	Turn off the computer and phone and find a place to be alone.

Chapter 8
Staying Awake

Have you ever decided you were going to spend more time in prayer and the next thing you know, you wake up from a sound sleep?

Me too.

My husband Jack works very hard operating a painting business, pastoring, and coaching high school track. I don't know how he does it all on the amount of sleep he gets. I do know he benefits from taking quick little naps. One time we were in a prayer meeting– I don't mean one with hundreds of people there, but just six of us in the room, seated in a circle. We were praying specifically for a man named Greg, who was one of the six. Next thing I know, I could see Jack's head had bowed, not in show of reverence, but in a napping pose. Since I was not seated next to him, I couldn't touch him and wake him, so I prayed a little louder, hoping it would rouse him. We were all listening to see if we would hear anything from the Lord for Greg. Within a few minutes, the leader checked to see if anyone had heard anything. This awakened Jack and he smiled from ear to ear and exclaimed, "Well, I fell asleep and had a dream about Greg." Jack now thinks he is free to fall asleep in prayer meetings! The problem for me is that when I fall asleep, I just fall asleep and nothing productive happens.

Fortunately, I am not the only one with this problem, as even the Bible speaks about this. "Then he came back to his three disciples and found them all sound asleep. He awakened Peter and said to him, 'Simon, are you asleep? Do you lack the strength to stay awake with me for even just an hour? Keep alert and pray that you'll be spared from this time of testing. For your spirit is eager enough, but your humanity is feeble'" (Mark 14:37–38, TPT).

Just like Peter in the Garden of Gethsemane, our spirit is often willing, maybe even excited to pray, but many times our flesh is weak. The Greek word "stay awake with me" or in some versions, "watch," is *gregoreuo*. It means to "watch; refrain from sleep." It denotes attention to God's revelation, a mindfulness of threatening dangers, which, with conscious earnestness and an alert mind, keeps one from all drowsiness and all slackening in the energy of faith and conduct."[1]

An alert mind keeps us from drowsiness and from slackening in faith and conduct. Alertness comes when we are fully aware of a situation that calls for our attention.

Just like the definition states, an alert mind keeps us from drowsiness and from slackening in faith and conduct. Alertness comes when we are fully aware of a situation that calls for our attention. For example, if we thought there was a thief trying to physically break into our house, we probably wouldn't fall asleep, but if it was a daily occurrence, we might. There is a thief coming to kill, steal, and destroy (see John 10:10), but because it is a daily occurrence, sleep can creep up on us. Without a doubt, we need to be fully aware of our partnership with Jesus and the importance of our prayers.

Without giving into fear, maybe we need to take a realistic look at what is happening around ourselves, our family, our city, and our nation. Many of us are like the ostrich, with our heads in the sand; we need to pull our heads out so that we can understand the urgency of the hour. If we doubt our prayers have an impact, then it is easier to fall asleep. We must understand the importance of our personal prayers. The Lord said in Ezekiel 22:30 that He was looking for a man to stand in the gap. Not a prayer group, a prayer chain, or a prayer meeting, just one person, and He couldn't find one. That gives us a sobering jolt to the value of our prayers. Maybe that will keep us alert and awake.

We also need to be fully aware of the partnership we walk in with Jesus. He didn't have to, but He chose to limit Himself to our partnership and agreement. He chooses to have us use our delegated authority. The tragedy of the fall in Genesis 3 was that Adam and Eve lost their authority over the enemy. The victory of the cross is that Jesus bought back our authority. Satan has always had power, but at the cross his authority was stripped. Satan will continue to use his power unless we as believers exercise the authority Jesus won for us. Dutch Sheets explains this in his excellent book, *Authority in Prayer: Praying with Power and Purpose.*

> The King James Version uses the Greek words dunamis (power) and exousia (authority) interchangeably, which is unfortunate and creates confusion. In Colossians 1:13, for example, it translates exousia as power, "Who hath delivered us from the power of darkness, and hath translated us into the kingdom of his dear Son." The verse should read that Christ has delivered us from the authority of darkness, as most other translations actually do. . . .
>
> This is more than a mere technicality. If Jesus stripped Satan of his power, as some teach, then we no longer need to concern ourselves with him—he becomes a nonissue. Or if we Christians have been delivered from Satan's power, as some teach, then he can no longer affect or control us. We would be able to ignore him completely, which is precisely what many Christians do.
>
> If on the other hand, Jesus dealt with Satan's authority—the right to use his power or abilities—then we would need to

deal with him as a usurper, a rebel, a thief that has no *right* to steal, kill and destroy but *will* if not stopped (see John 10:10). If we have been delivered from Satan's authority and given a higher authority in Christ's name, then we must exercise that authority over the devil's works and power. When we do, God's awesome power will back up our authority.[3]

When we pray for healing, we can pray for God to heal, but He also desires us to command the healing like Jesus did. When Moses stood at the Red Sea, if God was talking the way we talk, He would have said, "What are you waiting for? Deal with the sea! Use your authority!" (See Exodus 14:15–31).

Although these shifts in our mindsets may help us stay more alert, there are also some practical things we might do.

- Get plenty of sleep. You may be falling asleep because you're worn out and tired. Try going to sleep earlier if possible.
- Splash chilly water on your face. (I just recommend this; I don't do it!)
- Go for a walk and pray.
- Find a more uncomfortable place to pray. Most of us won't fall asleep in a dining room chair.
- Pray from a list; you may stay more focused and be less likely to fall asleep.
- Kneel when you pray.
- Pray out loud, most of us won't fall asleep while talking. My friend Alemu Beeftu would get up very early to pray. His children have fond memories of waking up to their dad's loud prayers.
- Use props to pray so more of your senses are involved. Maps, pictures, and little mementos might get you more involved.
- Experiment. Are you more or less likely to fall asleep with music?

- Adjust the heat. If I am cold, I will grab a blanket and shortly thereafter the prayer time ends, but maybe you are the type that won't fall asleep when you are cold.

When we fall asleep while praying, it is so easy to come under condemnation, but Romans 8:1 reminds us, "So now the case is closed. There remains no accusing voice of condemnation against those who are joined in life-union with Jesus, the Anointed One" (TPT). Condemnation doesn't help us change. In fact, it discourages us and causes us to think we are losers. Repent if needed but receive His forgiveness.

Father God,

Forgive us for not walking in the authority you have given us. We want to partner with you in prayer. We understand the importance of this, but we need your help. Help us to be alert. We want to be aware of what is going on around us without getting sucked into a media vortex. Our spirit is willing, but our flesh is weak. Help us. Let our spirits rise higher than our soul and body. Show us which practical ideas will work for us. In Jesus' Name, Amen.

Symptom	Potential Problem	Try this Solution
I keep falling asleep while I am praying.	You are physically tired, passion is waning, or you are not alert to the dangers around you.	Realize the authority God has granted you. Get rest. Try something different. Realize the gravity of the hour we are in.

Chapter 9
Small, Faithless Prayers

Often, our prayers are small and faithless because we only know a small, distant, uninvolved God. We read about experiences in the Bible and file it away as something that only happened in Bible times or the "olden days." If we are surrounded by those who also pray small, faithless prayers, we conclude this is what Christianity is all about. We tend to believe Christianity consists of being good and obeying the rules, which in many ways seems easier than following the mysterious ways of the Spirit.

In parts of the twenty-first century western Church, there is frequently a desire to weed out anything of mystery from the church. The problem is, God is mysterious. His ways are mysterious. We can't confine His ways to what fits our emotional or spiritual capacities.

Romans 11:33 states, "Oh, the depth of the riches and wisdom and knowledge of God! How unfathomable (inscrutable, unsearchable) are His judgments (His decisions)! And how untraceable (mysterious, undiscoverable) are His ways (His methods, His paths)!"(AMPC) As I pondered this verse, I was drawn to the word *inscrutable*, which is not a word we use much these days. After looking in several dictionaries, I would define *inscrutable* as something that is not easily understood or interpreted. It is, in fact, unfathomable. It cannot be understood by study, inquiry, or human reasoning. There are times we understand Him, His judgements, or His ways by revelation. We see the thread of the Spirit and what God is doing. Other times, it may take years to understand. Then there are some things we may have to accept as inscrutable.

We can pray for one person, and nothing happens. We can pray for the next person, and he or she receives a breakthrough. When we don't see a miracle and we take it upon ourselves to explain God, we can release shame on the person who didn't receive a miracle, or we explain God in a way that changes our theology to match our experience. We may try to put God in a box so we can understand Him, but when we can embrace the love and mystery of God, there is freedom.

Maybe that is why speaking in tongues is so controversial in some parts of the body of Christ. In some circles, you will not only lose your reputation but possibly your job or position in a church if you admit to speaking in tongues. Why? Good question. Is it because we don't understand it or can't control it? It is in the Word. "Therefore, my brethren, desire earnestly to prophesy, and do not forbid to speak in tongues" (1 Corinthians 14:39 NASB).

Can I explain the power of speaking in tongues? Not really. But I have seen it and experienced it. Many times, I don't know how to pray. So, I pray in the Spirit. Many times, I need my faith built up, so I pray in the Spirit (see Jude 20). When I need more power, I pray in the Spirit.

One might respond, "I have seen abuses with spiritual gifts and tongues." Even though we have seen people abuse money, sex, and food, we still want to experience these. Another person might add, "I don't know how it works." There are a lot of things we use, but we don't know how they function. Yet, we are very willing to use them. These include our phones, computers, and electronic tablets. We don't need to understand all the workings of something to use it. When we trust the maker of the gift, we trust the gift. When Samsung had trouble with their phone batteries catching on fire in 2016, this became a huge issue for the company, because it tarnished the trust their customers had in the maker of the phone. People were afraid to buy or use them.

When we give up control, we feel vulnerable. If we trust someone, we can be vulnerable with them. The issue with praying in tongues is we may feel out of control in our praying when we are not choosing our every word. We are not controlling what is being prayed, which in some ways is the beauty of a spiritual language; it takes us out of our mind and into our spirit. But we have to trust the Holy Spirit, who is praying through us.

The enemy loves to present authority figures, fathers, and Father God as not worthy of our trust. Frequently, we project the characteristics of our earthly fathers onto our Heavenly Father. If your dad was angry, is that how you see God? Indifferent or absent fathers many times cause us to think our Heavenly Father is the same. If, in our early life, the enemy can plant the seed that authority is untrustworthy, especially fathers, then when things become difficult, or in a season of waiting, our trust can wane to the point where we aren't willing to risk being vulnerable and asking for something in prayer. We may think we need to fix our prayer life, when in reality, we need to deal with our trust issues.

We may think we need to fix our prayer life, when in reality, we need to deal with our trust issues.

If we don't trust our Heavenly Father, it is difficult to be honest with Him. Certainly, we might be able to recite rote prayers, but baring our soul and genuinely desiring open communication where we honestly share our emotions and the challenges we face may feel too scary and vulnerable. We don't trust Him with our feelings, and we aren't sure if He wants what is best for us.

We mentored a young, single mom who moved to Colorado Springs on a bus with her three-year-old son. Melissa was radically saved, and we could see the life of Jesus in her. She came from a home with parents who, because of their own wounds, were not trustworthy. Abused as a young girl, her parents didn't believe her, even with physical evidence. She grew rapidly in the Lord, but she struggled with trust issues. When we, as her pastors, disappointed her, it seemed to solidify her view: Authority cannot be trusted. From that time on, she struggled in many ways, but it was usually rooted in the lie that authority, including God, could not be trusted.

How do we begin to deal with our trust issues? Sometimes, this might be as simple as coming out of agreement with the lie and declaring you trust your Heavenly Father. It could be that trust needs to be rebuilt through counseling or deliverance. Other times, it may take the transforming of your mind (see Romans 12:2) by meditating on the trustworthiness of God. Focus on His trustworthiness throughout Scripture. Remember all the times He has been faithful in your own life. Maybe even make a list of those times to keep handy for review.

Our friend Melody started coming to our church years ago. She was in the midst of a difficult time in her life. She had health issues, and her husband, a faithful veteran who had given much for our country, was now struggling with physical issues directly related to his service. The season in her life was changing, as her children were now young adults. She had been raised in a strict, religious home, but her father did not reflect our Heavenly Father. He was a harsh, rejecting man. It is no wonder she was struggling. A turning point came as she was about to have open heart surgery to replace a valve. We had been praying for her healing and praying faithfully for the surgery. Through no fault of her own, her surgery kept getting delayed. We could do nothing but keep praying.

Finally, the day of the surgery came, and it went well. We were all extremely thankful, but we didn't know how thankful until she recovered, came back to church, and testified. The doctor told her, "I don't know how you are alive. When I touched your heart valve it dissolved in my hand. It is amazing you are alive!" I believe it was the beginning of a shift for her. She could see the loving hand of the

Father and His care for her. She has worked hard to overcome some of the negative experiences of her past. She is always one of the first people I text when a prayer request comes in, and she serves as a personal intercessor for our family. I trust her to hear the voice of the Father and to pray bold, faith-filled prayers.

Do you trust the Lord to give you what you need? Yield your mind and emotions to your spirit. Have you asked Him for all he has to give? Reaffirm your trust in the Lord. When we trust Him, we can pray bold, faith-stretching prayers. Get to know our loving, awesome, unpredictable, powerful, and mysterious God.

Father God,

Forgive me for making you small in my eyes. I acknowledge your ways are higher than mine and your thoughts are higher than mine. I lay down my reputation and I yield myself to you. I want to trust you. Help me overcome those issues that are keeping me from trusting you. Help me to pray faith-filled prayers. Help me to have the courage to step out, be vulnerable, and ask with great faith for you to intervene in my situation. Give me great revelation and boldness as I pray for others. I choose to take my eyes off my circumstances and the areas where I see no movement, and instead to fix my eyes on my trustworthy Heavenly Father. I want to connect with others that are praying audacious prayers and seeing them answered. In Jesus' Name, Amen.

Symptom	Potential Problem	Try this Solution
I seem to be praying small, faithless prayers.	You may be unsure of who God is and how much He loves you, or you don't trust God.	Get to know Father God. Embrace the mystery and vastness of God.

Chapter 10
Where's the Hope?

I loved her, but I couldn't seem to reach her. She was overdiagnosed, overmedicated, and trapped in a world of hopelessness. Early onset dementia, or MS, or depression, or, or, or. She could barely bring the spoon to her mouth because her hand shook so much. She was a shell of her former self. I knew it wasn't the Lord's will.

I had prayed for years, but there was no change.

The Lord had given us a word to hold onto, but that took hope, and I had very little. "'But I will restore you to health and heal your wounds,' declares the LORD, 'because you are called an outcast, Zion for whom no one cares'" (Jeremiah 30:17). There had been no glimmer of hope.

I was busy with our six children, so I tried to stay focused on taking care of them. She was living but dead. She was there but missing. I prayed less and less for her. How could I quit praying for my own mother?

I knew something was wrong when I looked at our adorable nine-month-old and felt nothing. I had shut down my emotions. The problem with choosing not to feel something painful in one area is that you can't self-select. If you choose not to feel about one area, it shuts down your emotions everywhere.

I was living with a hope-deferred heart. Dutch Sheets, in his foundational work on hope deferred, *The Power of Hope*, states, "Hope deferred is the common cold of the soul."[1] Almost everyone deals with it at some time in their lives. It causes us to doubt the goodness of God. Prayers become rote and dry. Life becomes flat and gray, and our vision for the future is distorted.

But a hope-deferred heart does not need to be terminal. We can hope again. God hasn't left. He is no less faithful, no less powerful, no less willing. He is only hindered by our perspective. Our focus has shifted off the King of Kings and onto our problem. We have all dealt with difficult problems and circumstances. Don't hear me discount the pain, because the pain is real, whether it is the death of someone we love, a wandering child, a divorce or a loveless marriage, or dreams that don't materialize. Or, as Dutch eloquently says:

- a gallant fight of faith that was seemingly lost;
- as David experienced, false accusation, life in a cave and a seemingly lost destiny;
- as in Abraham's life, an Ishmael that God won't accept and an Isaac you can't produce.[2]

Hope deferred makes the heart sick, but a longing fulfilled is a tree of life (Proverbs 13:12).

When hope's dream seems to drag on and on, the delay can be depressing. But when at last your dream comes true, life's sweetness will satisfy your soul (Proverbs 13:12 TPT).

Oh, the anguish in the waiting! Doubt and despair love to come knocking in the time of waiting. But if we can wait with hope, waiting is not so bad. I heard once that next to suffering, God uses waiting the most to conform us to His image. In many ways, waiting without hope is suffering.

Just like there are stages of physical sickness, there are also levels of hope deferred. Many times, if we ignore minor sickness or injuries, they get more severe. This is true of hope deferred as well.

According to Dutch, this is the likely progression of unchecked hope deferred:

1. Discouragement, the early stage of this disease
2. Confusion, wherein we begin to question ourselves, our dreams and God's promises
3. Unbelief, wherein hope is lost, and expectation is gone
4. Disillusionment, the first stage of bitterness which usually involves questioning even the character of God
5. Bitterness, wherein with deep feelings of resentment we blame God, others and maybe even ourselves
6. Cynicism, a complete loss of faith and hope[3]

We need hope to function in this faith walk. "But those who hope in the LORD will renew their strength. They will soar on wings like eagles; they will run and not grow weary, they will walk and not be faint" (Isaiah 40:31).

Interestingly, the NIV translated the Hebrew word *qavah* as "hope," while other translations use "wait." There is a waiting, *qavah*, that is intertwined with hope and brings renewed strength, but if we are waiting without hope, it is easy to get into hope deferred.

If we run without hope, hope deferred can distort our vision, making our enemies and problems loom large and our attributes appear small and weak. In Dutch's original book on hope deferred, *Tell Your Heart to Beat Again*, he points out that functioning from a hope-deferred heart can cause us to run, with an increased risk for running in ways that are not pleasing to God. We are going to look at how Dutch says we may run (these are the boldface titles)[4] and I will reframe them to address how this affects our lives, especially our prayer lives.

1. Run Ahead Of God

When we are waiting on God and seeing others having success, producing fruit, or getting accolades, the waiting becomes more difficult, especially if we are under pressure to produce something. Think of Abraham and Sarah. They believed what God said to them about their descendants. "He took him outside and said, 'Look up at the sky and count the stars—if indeed you can count them.' Then he said to him, 'So shall your offspring be.' Abram believed the LORD, and he credited it to him as righteousness" (Genesis 15:5-6).

After the delivery of this glorious promise, they had to wait and wait, and at the same time, live in their old bodies as a daily reminder of their unanswered prayers. The temptation when we see no movement is to make something happen. Whatever our prayer is for, we do all we can to make it come forth. Sarah, in all likelihood, hopeless and in despair, chose to send Hagar to Abraham (see Genesis 16). Making things happen rarely works to our benefit in this walk of faith. This temptation to make our prayers produce results can cause us to parent young adults like we would an eight-year-old, harm relationships with control, and be tempted to use money or words to manipulate people or situations. These are only three of many pitfalls which can occur when we step into the trap of running ahead of God.

2. Run Away From God

Hope deferred can cause us to run away from our destiny and anything or anyone that reminds us of God. A good example of this is when, after the death and resurrection of Jesus, Peter told the other disciples that he was going fishing. This wasn't like it is today, where people go fishing to relax and refresh. He was running from what he didn't understand. He chose to go back to his old life of fishing.

Many still pray as they run away from God because it is a habit, or they are afraid of not praying for their families. They may pray because it is part of their job (whether volunteer or paid) but it will be a "religious" form of praying. There won't be much intimacy in these prayer times. We can't pursue intimacy with God while running away from Him.

3. Run From Our Enemies.

Hope-deferred hearts may become battle weary and full of fear. Our hearts can cause us to doubt ourselves and even doubt God. Does He really love me? Does He even know or care what is happening to me and my family? Instead of choosing to move forward in faith and believing the Word that describes us as more than a conqueror (see Romans 8:37), we tend to operate in fear and timidity, running from our adversaries.

We may become like the Israelites when Moses led them toward the Promised Land. As they faced the unknown and waited without a breakthrough, even though there had been miracles in their recent past, they wanted to go back to Egypt. Their vision became distorted, and they longed for the familiar, seemingly forgetting that what was familiar to them was bondage. We, like the Israelites, also may choose to go back to our Egypt. We may run back to old familiar places where we find comfort, like alcohol, food, binge watching, Facebook, Instagram, TikTok, or whatever our favorite way of numbing is. Sometimes people will also avoid their battles by jumping into a new job, a new marriage, new church, or anyplace new where they can escape the battles of the old.

If Satan can deceive us into thinking we can make peace with him and he will leave us alone, we have just become his unwitting victim, and he wins by our surrender.

The problem is, everywhere they go, there they are with their hope-deferred heart.

How does this affect the way we pray? We want to stay where we are comfortable and try to avoid any type of battle. Unfortunately, we are born on a battlefield of good versus evil. Concerning the battle with the enemy, we declare, "I'll leave you alone if you leave me alone." The dilemma we face with this mindset is that the enemy is a liar and has no mercy. If he can deceive us into thinking we can make peace with him and he will leave us alone, we have just become his unwitting victim, and he wins by our surrender. We end up praying "safe" prayers that hopefully don't attract the attention of the enemy, but these prayers limit our partnership with the Lord, who describes himself as the "Commander of the army of the Lord" (see Joshua 5:14, NKJV).

4. Run Religiously Without Power.

When the going gets tough, the religious work harder! The Israelites had been waiting for the Messiah for so long; they were oppressed and though praying, nothing seemed to shift. This is a classic environment for hope-deferred hearts to develop and such an easy place to step into religious striving. This is where we find Pharisee-like people obeying every letter of the law with no joy and no life.

If we are honest, many of us can identify with going through religious motions and praying from a place of duty instead of intimacy. It is easy to step from that place into performance and praying to be seen while getting our validation from others praising our many-worded prayers. No fruit to our prayer life except being seen. The other end of the religious striving spectrum is to live under the condemnation of thinking our prayers are never good enough. It is all about measuring. Either I compare myself to "worse" pray-ers and feel pride at my eloquent prayers, or I measure against those who seem to get their prayers answered more frequently and suffer under the condemnation.

5. Run With God's Enemies.

This is the most extreme case. Judas, one of Jesus' disciples, was so disappointed and probably hope deferred, because Jesus wasn't taking over governmentally, that he devised a way to profit from betraying Jesus.

I wish I could say that I can't imagine a person would even pray from this place, but there was a time in my life where I was so wounded and hurt, my hope-deferred condition had not only moved in but had decorated for a long stay. I walked in unforgiveness, bitterness, and deception, and yet I still prayed. When we are deceived like this, the enemy will plant his ideas and schemes in the demonic strongholds in our minds, which lines up with that bitter place in our hearts. A person can pray wicked things without even comprehending they are in the presence of a Holy God. When someone is deceived, praying prayers of bitterness and control is tragic but not impossible.

Don't despair from any of these places. God is a covenant-keeping God who longs to heal, forgive, and help restore us to living in hope.

Dear Lord,

Search me, O God, and see my heart. Show me any place I am hope deferred. Let me see myself from a place of clarity. Give me a teachable heart. Show me any place I am running. I want to be a hope-filled overcomer. In Jesus' Name, Amen.

Symptom	Potential Problem	Try this Solution
I can't seem to pray. I have no hope.	You may be hope deferred.	Recognize the symptoms of hope deferred.

Chapter 11

Overcoming Hope Deferred

Choose hope. This seems almost simplistic, but much of the gospel is simple without being simplistic or easy.

Choose hope. This seems almost simplistic, but much of the gospel is simple without being simplistic or easy.

Simple and easy are not synonymous in the spiritual realm. I have a choice whether to stay in despair or to hope. I have a choice of who I put my hope in. "When everything was hopeless, Abraham believed anyway, deciding to live not on the basis of what he saw he *couldn't* do but on what God said he *would* do" (Romans 4:18, MSG, emphasis added). This is one of my favorite passages in the Bible. Frequently, we focus on our circumstances and what is not working "right" in our lives. Abraham had the same temptation, but he chose to believe what God said. We have the same choice.

We can't assume we can take this journey alone. When we are struggling in our spiritual journey, we tend to self-isolate. We find ourselves in a pit and decide to dig ourselves out alone. Sadly, we may not have the tools to dig ourselves out. Find someone who has a spiritual shovel and ask them to either give you the shovel or dig you out. Maybe others have a ladder they can lower into the pit, which enables you to get out one step at a time. First, we must be humble enough to admit we are in a pit, and second, we must be humble enough to receive help and counsel.

When isolated, people are vulnerable to the lies of the enemy. They may also attribute insights to God that He did not and would never say. We are susceptible to deception when all alone. This is one reason we need others in our life. Most of us have people we can call who will take our side, give us advice, and commiserate with us. In contrast, we are blessed if we have one or two friends on speed dial who will give us a listening ear, share a verse with us, pray for us, pray with us in agreement, speak the truth in love, or listen to the Lord on our behalf. We need someone who can tell us we are believing a lie of the enemy, or what we *think* God said doesn't sound like Him at all. We need friends who are willing to share their tools with us.

Recently, I prayed for a woman who had faced great disappointment and hopelessness. It made me realize the feelings of vulnerability that surface when reopening oneself to hope and seeking help. Finding the courage to believe once more is challenging, especially for those who, in the past, had extended their faith believing that God would respond. However, as the waiting persisted, they eventually lost hope. It's crucial that we rediscover hope, but doing so requires embracing vulnerability once again—being open to the possibility of experiencing pain in order to reach eventual victory.

I get it; it's scary.

We have a choice of who we agree with. We can agree with the lover of our soul or the enemy of our soul. Romans 15:13 describes God as the "God of hope." He is the actual source of our hope. Come out of agreement with hopelessness and the enemy of your soul. It is tempting to just let thoughts wander around in our minds without taking thoughts captive. We need to ask if this thought lines up with the Word of God. If it doesn't line up, then it doesn't belong in my mind. Build up the strength of your inner core by meditating on or memorizing scriptures that build faith and hope in your inner being. This is not a one-time event, but a process. Replacing what we have been thinking with what the Lord says is vital to this process. When we have been living in a state of hope deferred, our thoughts have lined up with the hope deferred. Negative, hopeless, and depressed thoughts are normal for us. Now, we need to transform our minds into thinking that lines up with the Word of God, words that are full of hope. "Don't copy the behavior and customs of this world, but let God transform you into a new person by changing the way you think" (Romans 12:2, NLT).

Being aware of how hope deferred works can help us the next time we wander down the path of hopelessness. We can choose to deal with it in the early stages instead of waiting until we are entrenched in hopelessness and have become cynical and bitter. This works together with watching over our hearts, which I discuss in Chapter 27.

Back to my mom's struggle with her health and my hope-deferred life. She was in her sixties, living in a nursing home, incredibly weak, and hardly recognizable. After walking in hope deferred for quite some time, I explained her situation to Doris Wagner, a national leader in prayer, deliverance, and spiritual warfare. She advised, "I think your only hope is to pray for a miracle." I had just enough faith to utter a few prayers, asking God to do a miracle for my mom. My husband, Jack, continued to pray for her regularly.

Not too long after that, I received a phone call from my dad. Mom was in the hospital. She had suffered a massive stroke. They weren't sure she would live. I drove the three hours to the hospital, wondering and kind of praying. It looked really bad. They were discussing whether to give her a feeding tube.

Again, I found myself in a numb place. A good friend stopped by the hospital. I admitted I didn't even know how to pray. She replied, "I think God is always pleased when we pray for life." So, I did.

Mom was in what I would call "an awake state with no one home." We would look at her, and she would look at us, but with no recognition or response. As I was with my mom that same afternoon, a young aide came bebopping into mom's room with a plate of meatloaf, mashed potatoes and gravy, and green beans. The sweet young volunteer aide started feeding Mom. I kept thinking somebody should do something, but I didn't know what to do and my dad, who was also in the room, didn't seem to know what to do either. So, Mom, in whatever state she was in, ate mashed potatoes and meatloaf. About an hour after the meal was over, a technician came in and informed us that they were going to do a swallow test to see if she could swallow. We looked at each other, knowing something had happened out of order. We explained that someone came in and fed her mashed potatoes and meatloaf. Without thinking, the tech declared, "No, that is dangerous. She could choke to death!" After realizing that was not a good thing to say to family in this litigious society, he left the room.

We never heard any more discussion about feeding tubes. We also didn't see the aide again. Either she was asked not to come back, or she was an angel! That was the beginning of the miracle. In the next few days, while in that state, she detoxed off all the medication and came out of it in her right mind. Her assisted living home, run by believers, took her back home and helped her rehab. She recovered from all the stroke's effects on her right side. She learned to walk again, and essentially, we received our mom back from the dead.

Let's acknowledge that not everyone gets this great answer. Unfortunately, moms die. I get that. But there are some lessons to learn. First, when seeking advice from Doris Wagner, I humbled myself to seek help. Her advice gave us a glimmer of hope. That little bit of hope helped to raise my head out of hope deferred long enough to pray some prayers of faith. Also, I was not walking through this alone. Jack and other family members were walking through this with me.

If you've experienced the loss of a loved one or gone through a divorce, your path out of being hope deferred may look different. This is because you are also navigating the grieving process in addition to choosing to hope again. I'll defer advice on dealing with grief to the experts, but I want to emphasize that for those in grief, overcoming hope deferred may be a significant aspect of your journey.

There is one other area where we need to watch out for hope deferred. Many of us have learned about the authority that God wants us to walk in with our prayer life. We have seen Him partner with us. He has shown us his will. We have decreed it and seen it come to pass. It is so wonderful. But the danger of knowing this type of authority is that we can forget the crucial step of listening and hearing what He desires, and instead start decreeing and declaring what our own soul desires. This can be dangerous to our own hearts, but when we do this as leaders, we create an atmosphere that is ripe for hope deferred to be released over many. Leaders decree something with great passion, but from their own will. What they decree doesn't come to pass, young, inexperienced, and even mature believers can easily conclude, "This doesn't work! If Brother Wonderful can't get this to work, there must be no hope for me." This has created a great deal of hope deferred across the body of Christ.

Dear Father,

Forgive me for any place I have stepped into hope deferred. I choose to come out of agreement with hopelessness. I shut the door to any demonic forces that have taken advantage of this open door. I choose to believe again. Give me strength to hope again. I choose to believe more in what I know You can do than what I see with my eyes. In Jesus' name, Amen.

Symptom	Potential Problem	Try this Solution
I can't seem to pray or I am praying lifeless prayers.	You may not know how to overcome hope deferred.	Recognize the problem. Receive healing. Choose to hope again.

Chapter 12
Disappointment

I made a snarky comment, which revealed some cynicism in my heart. We were discussing God's ability to supply what we need with some friends who were businesspeople. I didn't think they understood our struggle with our calling, thus the snarky comment. The hostess noticed. I noticed the hostess notice. It wasn't long before she said, "We need to pray for Jack and Terri."

I knew I was busted. I am usually on the other end of the busting. We had lived by faith for years where God met our every need, but there wasn't much abundance. Now we were pastoring bi-vocationally. There had been a struggle as my husband went through a transition from "I am called to full-time ministry," to "Everything I do can be under the umbrella of full-time ministry, whether I am leading a church, coaching young people, or running a painting business." Our finances seemed to fluctuate with his mindset.

As we entered the prayer time, they asked what we needed. It was difficult to extend my faith for the material things we needed. These weren't desires. They were needs. I had been driving a car without air-conditioning for two years, which isn't a huge deal in Colorado, if you could get the windows open, but only one window would open. The bright Colorado sun can really heat up a car even in the winter. We also needed a new mattress for our bed. If they had asked me what I thought the city needed, I could have stated with great faith what was needed.

Some could have said, "Oh Terri, you have a poverty mindset and maybe even a spirit of poverty." They could have prayed about it, and we might still be waiting. Allowing the Holy Spirit to reveal what a person is dealing with is essential.

Following the prayer time, one of the guys, Ted, pulled us aside and asked us some questions. I call it my "Ted Talk." As we pondered and answered his questions, it was clear I was dealing with disappointment, and specifically a spirit of disappointment. Disappointment is a normal emotion we can have over a circumstance, but when the enemy takes advantage of our normal emotions and attaches to them in a demonic way, establishing a stronghold, we then are dealing with a spirit of disappointment (or whatever emotion he is attaching to). There at the table, I prayed, "Lord, forgive me for being disappointed in You and not trusting You. I choose to place my trust in You. I speak to a spirit of disappointment and tell you to go. I call in a spirit of faith to replace any place where the spirit of disappointment was."

It was interesting because it was as if my heart was divided. I had great faith in some areas but had opened a door to disappointment in other areas. Over time, if left alone, this disappointment would have taken over more of my heart. The good news is within a few weeks, we had a new mattress and a new used car without going into debt.

The Bible tells us, "Behold, I lay in Zion a choice stone, a precious cornerstone, and he who believes in Him will not be disappointed" (1 Peter 2:6 NASB). There are several times a similar passage occurs in the Scriptures; some say "hopes," and some say "believes," but the truth to grab ahold of is if we find ourselves in a place of disappointment, we need to acknowledge we may not be hoping and believing in Him. It guides us back to the root issue so we can deal with it.

How can you tell you are in a place of disappointment?

Here are some typical symptoms of disappointment:

- Sadness, self-pity, or maybe even depression
- Comparing ourselves to others from the place of disappointment
- Not praying in the area of our life in which disappointment resides
- Angry or snarky comments
- Quitting
- A feeling of being oppressed by our enemies

As Dana Candler, a Bible teacher, intercessor, and author, explains in her book *First Love,* "Our paths and circumstances all vary, but the results are often much the same. Whether our story is riddled with broken relationships, financial difficulties, sickness, or prodigal children, inward offense is often the outcome. God, where are You? God, why? We struggle to trust the Lord with our losses, our hearts weighed down with grief. God, how could You allow this to happen? Disillusionment can set in when things don't play out as we had hoped or when our failures slam us against the wall of disappointment."[4]

> *When we see disappointment, it helps us seek out the situations where we have quit trusting.*

Where have we quit trusting? When we see disappointment, it helps us seek out the situations where we have quit trusting. In Psalm 42, David lets us inside his thoughts as he struggles with disappointment.

> Day and night my tears keep falling
> and my heart keeps crying for your help
> while my enemies mock me over and over, saying,
> "Where is this God of *yours*? Why doesn't he help you?"

> So I speak over my heartbroken soul,
> "Take courage. Remember when you used to be

right out front leading the procession of praise
when the great crowd of worshipers
gathered to go into the presence of the Lord?
You shouted with joy as the sound of passionate celebration
filled the air and the joyous multitude of lovers
honored the festival of the Lord!"

So then, my soul, why would you be depressed?
Why would you sink into despair?
Just keep hoping and waiting on God, your Savior.
For no matter what, I will still sing with praise,
for living before his face is my saving grace!

Here I am depressed and downcast.
Yet I will still remember you as I ponder the place
where your glory streams down from the mighty moun-
taintops, lofty and majestic—*the mountains of your awesome
presence.*

My deep need calls out to the deep kindness of your love.
Your waterfall of weeping sent waves of sorrow
over my soul, carrying me away,
cascading over me like a thundering cataract.

Yet all day long God's promises of love pour over me.
Through the night I sing his songs,
For my prayer to God has become my life.

I will say to God, "You are my mountain of strength;
how could you forget me?
Why must I suffer this vile oppression of my enemies—
these heartless tormentors who are out to kill me?"

Their wounding words pierce my heart
over and over while they say,
"Where is this God of yours?"

So I say to my soul,
"Don't be discouraged. Don't be disturbed.

For I know my God will break through for me."
Then I'll have plenty of reasons to praise him all over again.
Yes, living before his face is my saving grace (Psalm 42:3-11
TPT).

David explains his situation which is full of difficulty and people who are mocking him. Then he speaks to his inner man and
reminds himself to "take courage," or "don't be discouraged," or he
declares, "yet, I will still remember You."

David is a great example of being real about the hard situation and not living in the land of denial, yet acknowledges God is
worthy of our trust. I love the way Brian Simmons says it in the
Passion Translation, "Yes, He is my saving grace!" Yes, things are
difficult, but I choose not to focus on my circumstances and what is
not happening and instead live in His presence, focusing on Him.
If we could just remember this! Our circumstances can be all we
see, but when we get into His presence, living before his face, our
circumstances quiet themselves as we listen for the voice of the One
we love.

Please don't hear me say that we are to live this life without
disappointment. We would have to be plastic and unfeeling to do
that. If we are honest, we will face disappointment with ourselves,
our spouse, our children, other loved ones, our church family, our
work associates, and our government. The key is to acknowledge
this quickly and realize our hope needs to be in the Lord. If we
think people will fill the void in our life and never disappoint, we
are wrong. Only God can fill that void. No person, position, situation, or thing is above causing us disappointment. If we trust Him,
we won't be disappointed.

Often, the disappointment comes when He delays His answer.
During the delay, we can start to doubt, fear, and then accuse God.
We are now *in* disappointment. We need to remember that though
we wait, God's character is not changed in the waiting, but ours can
be changed for our good if we choose to rest in the faithfulness of

God. "That is why waiting does not diminish us, any more than waiting diminishes a pregnant mother. We are enlarged in the waiting" (Romans 8:25 MSG). We continue to hold our desires with open hands as we ask God the Father to help us see the bigger picture.

There was a time when it took me years to see the bigger picture concerning our housing situation. Jack worked for a church where he was doing a great job and was well-loved as an associate pastor. We were being underpaid by most standards of the day, but we loved the church, and they loved us. At that time, we were living in a rental house. It was sold, and we had one month to find a place to live. At the same time, the long-time pastor and his wife decided to move out of the parsonage and move into a home of their own so they could build up equity for their retirement. Wow, it seemed like perfect timing! Except... The committee in charge of renting out the fully-paid-for parsonage saw this as an opportunity to make some money for the church. They met with Jack and said if we would put down two months' rent and then pay rent that was substantially more than what we were now paying (which was already a little tight), we could rent the parsonage. We financially could not do this, and yes, we were disappointed.

Others who knew our situation went to the leaders of our church and questioned why we weren't in the parsonage. This only led the leadership to accuse us of trying to stir up trouble. As you can imagine, this was a very difficult time for us. On the day before we had to move out of our house, we did find a place to live, but it had rooms that my 6'6" tall husband could not stand upright in. After spending a hot summer there with no air conditioning and only two bedrooms, we moved into a house with no hallways. It just went room to room to room. After a while, Mike and Pam Grassley, wonderful church members, came to us and offered to contract a house for us for free. We would pay for the supplies; we would work on it, and Mike would get church members to help work on it as well. We were excited, but we told Mike at the time that we weren't sure we were called to be in this community long term, as we had been feeling a call to move west. Mike graciously responded, "That's okay, if your next place has a parsonage, you will have a nest egg. If not, you will have a down payment for a house." He gave us a book of plans and let us graciously adapt them to fit our family. Then many, including ourselves, did a lot of hard work and we had a beautiful five-bedroom house for our family of eight.

Many came to us and rejoiced with us over this new house. We rejoiced too, thinking God had redeemed the uncharitable way we had been treated in the past. It took me many, many years to be able to see the full picture. God had an assignment for us in Colorado Springs. We wouldn't realize the fullness of the calling for years. We wouldn't have been able to move here and afford to buy a house if Mike and Pam hadn't been so generous. God knew that we would need to move here by faith (working for a church for $100 a week, plus health insurance), and in a few years He would need to shift us to a different stream in the body of Christ. In times of instability, the equity in the house helped us to survive. If we had moved into the beautiful parsonage, I wonder if Mike and Pam would have made the same offer? All those years I thought the enemy had borrowed those fine men on that committee, when in reality it was God's hand involved.

Often, we get disappointed with the Lord because we can't see the big picture.

Often, we get disappointed with the Lord because we can't see the big picture. We need to trust Him, knowing He loves us, knowing he is working things together for our good.

"So, we are convinced that every detail of our lives is continually woven together for good, for we are his lovers who have been called to fulfill his designed purpose" (Romans 8:28 TPT).

Heavenly Father,

Show me any place I have allowed disappointment to come into my heart. I want to trust You. I want to live in Your presence, where Your grace enables me to live to my fullest. I don't want to live my life under my circumstances, and I don't want to judge my life based on what I see with my physical eyes. I trust You. You are worthy of trust. I say it again: I trust You. In Jesus' Name, Amen.

Symptom	Potential Problem	Try this Solution
I have quit praying in certain areas of life. I don't trust God.	You may be living in disappointment or under the influence of a spirit of disappointment.	Recognize the problem. Admit the problem. Trust God. Deal with demonic attachments.

Troubleshooting Guide For Knowing How to Pray

Symptom	Potential Problem	Try this Solution	Chapter
I keep getting distracted when trying to pray.	Lack of quiet and too many distractions.	Turn off the computer and phone and find a place to be alone	7
I keep falling asleep while I am praying.	You are physically tired, passion is waning, or you are not alert to the dangers around you.	Realize the authority God has granted you. Get rest. Try something different. Realize the gravity of the hour we are in.	8
It seems like I am praying small, faithless prayers.	You may be unsure of who God is and how much He loves you or you don't trust God.	Get to know Father God. Embrace the mystery and vastness of God.	9
I can't seem to pray. I have no hope.	You may be hope deferred.	Recognize the symptoms of hope deferred.	10

I can't seem to pray, or I am praying lifeless prayers.	You may not know how to overcome hope deferred.	Receive healing. Choose to hope again.	11
I have quit praying in certain areas of life. I don't trust God.	You may be living in disappointment or under the influence of a spirit of disappointment.	Recognize the problem and admit it. Trust God. Deal with demonic attachments.	12

Unanswered Prayer

Chapter 13
Mixture

I was angry about our situation, and I was angry at a person I held responsible for it. I felt this spiritual leader should have handled the circumstances better. Nothing seemed fair, and I allowed my anger to fester to bitterness. I was still involved in prayer and teaching others the Bible. From the outside, I may have appeared godly, but on the inside bitterness and cynicism controlled much of my life, including my prayers. I had a stronghold of anger, and I was praying from that place. Sure, I still loved Jesus. Sure, I still knew the Scriptures. But there was a mixture that tainted my prayers.

I don't like to think of the Bible as a list of dos and don'ts, but as a love letter from my loving Father to be read with the guidance of the Holy Spirit. That said, there are principles laid out in Scripture for our good. If we live contrary to what He says, there are consequences. My unwillingness to forgive, which was contrary to the teaching of the Word, led to bitterness, and a Holy God could not answer my prayers. My prayers aligned more with what the enemy desired than what God desired. When we are living our lives in mixture, that is, when we adhere to some biblical principles, but combine it with our opinions, our disobedience, sometimes even our wounds, we end up praying from a place of mixture that can definitely affect whether a loving God can answer our prayers. After being set free of the bitterness, I was so grateful the Lord didn't answer those bitter "prayers."

There are several verses in Scripture that specifically speak of things that will hinder our prayers. "Husbands, you in turn must treat your wives with tenderness, viewing them as feminine partners who deserve to be honored, for they are co-heirs with you of the 'divine grace of life,' *so that nothing will hinder your prayers"* (1 Peter 3:7 TPT, emphasis added). If our prayers are hindered, by definition there could be a delay, interruption, or difficulty in the answer to our prayers. The warning is clear to husbands, but in our modern times, I wonder if we need to expand the warning to anyone who doesn't honor their spouse or doesn't see them as a co-heir to all the grace God has for us. In the culture this was written to, women were many times not honored. Unfortunately, many women do not honor their husbands as "co-heirs to the divine grace of life." They declare or live from the premise their husbands aren't spiritual enough, they don't spend enough time with the Lord, and further complaints. Some of this may be true, but a husband may commune with God differently than his spouse, and it could be the husband feels those judgments and has decided not to share his spiritual life with his wife. We all can benefit by searching our hearts and examining our behavior.

There are also three admonitions in the book of James concerning concerning answered prayer. The first deals with doubt:

> Just make sure you ask empowered by confident faith without doubting that you will receive. For the ambivalent person believes one minute and doubts the next. Being undecided makes you become like the rough seas driven and tossed by the wind. You're up one minute and tossed down the next. When you are half-hearted and wavering it leaves you unstable. Can you really expect to receive anything from the Lord when you're in that condition? (James 1:6-8 TPT)

Doubt will keep our prayers from being answered, so war against doubt. We can also be honest like the father who declared, "Lord, I believe; help my unbelief? (Mark 9:24 NKJV)

The next two admonitions come in James 4. "And all the time you don't obtain what you want because you won't ask God for it! James 4:2 TPT). Wow, we just need to be bold enough to ask for what we need or want. Are we walking with orphan mindsets that cause us to doubt our worthiness and cause us to not ask? He is telling us to just ask! What we ask for is not based on our goodness or our ability to keep a covenant but on His goodness and the truth that He is a covenant-keeping God.

Next, the intentions of our hearts can hinder the Lord from answering our prayers. "You ask and do not receive, because you ask with wrong motives, so that you may spend it on your pleasures" (James 4:3 NASB).

> *Are we walking with orphan mindsets that cause us to doubt our worthiness and cause us to not ask? He is telling us to just ask!*

Sometimes, we have blind spots concerning our motives and we need to ask the Lord to reveal our inner agenda. As David prayed, "God, I invite your searching gaze into my heart. Examine me through and through; find out everything that may be hidden within me. Put me to the test and sift through all my anxious cares" (Psalm 139:23 TPT).

Isaiah 58 confronts us for fulfilling religious duties like prayer and fasting, while ignoring the poor and taking advantage of our workers. "'Why have we fasted,' they say, 'and you have not seen it? Why have we humbled ourselves, and you have not noticed?' Yet on the day of your fasting, you do as you please and exploit all your workers" (Isaiah 58:3).

This is a different kind of mixture, but still a mixture. We do our religious duty to try to get God to alleviate our concern, but we turn a blind eye to those who are suffering around us. Again, this would give biblical ground to our prayers not being answered. How do we fix this? Get in a quiet place with the Lord and read through Isaiah 58 slowly. Ask the Lord to convict you where you need convicting, challenge you where you need challenging, and encourage you where you need encouragement.

Father God,

I desire to obey your Word. Please show me anywhere I am hindering the answer to my prayers by mixing my ways with Your ways. Give me grace to see the blind spots in my life or bring other loving people into my life to help me see those blind spots. In Jesus' Name, Amen.

Symptom	Potential Problem	Try this Solution
My prayers are not being answered.	Believing or living contrary to Scripture.	Change your mindsets or behavior.

Chapter 14
No Faith in the Atmosphere

Throughout the Gospels, we see very few times when Jesus couldn't do what He set out to do. Matthew 13:58 states, "And he did not do many miracles there because of their lack of faith." We don't know exactly how He was hindered by their lack of faith, but we know Jesus did not do many miracles there. We can conclude that their lack of faith created an atmosphere that hindered Him.

Instead of asking the hard questions about why we aren't seeing miracles, many just change their theology to say Jesus and Christians don't do miracles anymore. This does not hold up when you look at the fullness of the word of God: "Very truly I tell you, whoever believes in me will do the works I have been doing, and they will do even greater things than these, because I am going to the Father" (John 14:12). We were created to walk in the miraculous, but many of us don't. Does it ever bother you? Do you ever wonder why?

Are we creating an atmosphere of faith? How do we do that? One way we can create an atmosphere of faith is to release testimonies of how God is working miracles. Now! – not just in Biblical times but now. (I think testimonies from even one hundred years ago can create that atmosphere too.) The Hebrew word *ud*, meaning "to repeat" or "do it again" is translated as "testify."[1] As we testify of a miracle, we are declaring, "God, do it again!"

The more we release testimonies, the more people extend their faith. We saw this clearly in a Baptist church northeast of Kansas City. One of the dear women of God was sick with cancer, and the church fasted and prayed for her healing. She died, but in her death, a seed of healing was released that saw many, many people healed over the next several years, including two of our children. As the testimony of each healing was released, faith grew. If God healed Trish, then surely God could heal me. There was no Brother or Sister Wonderful that received the credit for the healings. The deacons anointed the sick with oil and laid hands on the sick, but the whole congregation also prayed, so no person got the credit, just Jesus. There was an atmosphere of healing and the miraculous in the house.

Sharon was a member of that church and a great friend. She and her husband were raising a young grandson. Sharon ran a small daycare, and they had transformed the garage into a room that her daycare could use. She would go up and down the three steps many times a day, but one day, she fell onto the cement floor and broke both of her wrists. Although she received proper medical care and received a measure of healing, the doctors told her she would never be able to turn her hands from palms down to palms up. One Sunday morning, Sharon was joyfully singing in the worship choir. She wasn't one of the lead singers on the microphone, just part of the choir. As she worshiped in the choir loft, suddenly she could move her hands just as the doctor said she would never be able to do. No one laid hands on her. No one was specifically praying from the microphone for her healing. There was an atmosphere of faith that enabled the miraculous to occur.

What we bring to a meeting affects the atmosphere. We may think our beliefs, attitudes, and actions have no effect on the corporate meeting. Not so. In larger congregations, it might be difficult to tell what is affecting what or who is affecting whom. During a ninety-day period in 2008, we belonged to a church that hosted the presence of God. Before I continue, let's look at the two aspects of God's presence identified in the Bible. The first is His omnipresence. David explains "I can never get away from your Spirit! If I go up to heaven, you are there; if I go down to the grave, you are there . . . Even in darkness I cannot hide from you." Psalm 139:7–8, 12 (NLT). This is His presence that is always with us. We see the other type in Jesus' statement, "I will love him and manifest Myself to him" (John 14:21 NKJV). The word "manifest" is translated from the Greek word *emphanizo*, and means, "to appear, reveal, be conspicuous."[2] There are times that God chooses, in His sovereignty and His mercy, to manifest in a meeting or to a small group or even with an individual. This occurred for ninety days at our church. People were there twenty-four hours a day, sometimes in large numbers and sometimes just a few. One time, my husband and I were there in the middle of the night with just three or four people in the room. God's presence was tangible. As we were worshiping with our eyes closed, we noticed a difference. We opened our eyes, glanced at each other, and looked around. Sure enough, someone had entered the room and shifted the atmosphere. The person didn't bring evil into the room, just busyness and distraction. If we can affect the atmosphere negatively, surely, we can influence the atmosphere positively as well.

How does an atmosphere of faith affect our prayer life? I've been in two different churches where women covenanted together to pray in faith for their husbands, who didn't know Jesus. In both cases, men started coming to the Lord. When one would get saved, the faith level would rise, and then they would pray with more diligence and faith, and another would get saved. An atmosphere of faith makes a difference. Surrounding ourselves by faith-filled people who are seeing God move in their lives and receiving answers to prayers, creates an atmosphere of faith that we can tap into. In contrast, if we surround ourselves with skeptics, complainers, whiners, and fear mongers, one can imagine the type of atmosphere created.

Although we all might describe ourselves as people of faith, we also need to acknowledge there are measures of faith and even distinct types of believers. James Goll, an author, speaker, and prophetic voice explained three different types of believers in a Facebook Live. The first group are those who honor the Word of God and believe everything written in the Word is true. They believe in the God of the past. The second group believes in the prophetic. They believe in the written promises of God and also those things that have been prophesied. They believe in the God of the future. The last group is a group that is arising. They honor the past and believe the word of God, they also believe the prophetic promises of God, but they want to pull it into the now. Faith is in the *now*!

When we pray for healing, we aren't asking God to heal them when He takes them to heaven, although He does that. We are asking for healing now. When we are in an atmosphere of faith, we are praying for our prodigals and being like the father in Luke 15, out looking for their return. Faith is active, and we exercise our faith when we have a confident hope God is hearing us and responding to our prayers.

God is not a God of rules, but of relationship in the midst of mystery.

We also need to acknowledge that when and where God chooses to heal is a mystery. Sometimes it seems obvious to us, in our way of measuring, there has not been enough prayer or the right kind of prayer. We think surely God will not act here. There are also times where there is such a concerted effort in prayer by amazing prayer warriors, we think surely God will heal in this situation. It is not as simple as meeting some prayer threshold, and then God will perform. It is inscrutable and sometimes frustrating, because if we just knew the rules, we would play by them! God is not a God of rules, but of relationship in the midst of mystery. Our best hope is to press into Him with the desire to know Him more.

Recently, in Colorado Springs, a church was preparing to host a grand reopening. They had been out of their church building for about eighteen months as the church was remodeled because the roof had been ripped off the building by destructive winds. (Not just the shingles, but the actual roof.) A long-time member of the church was in hospice the day before the grand reopening. Lola had been to Israel thirty years earlier, and both her wrists were healed at the wailing wall. From that time, she knew she walked in a healing anointing, but she never really exercised the gift fully. Lying in hospice on a Saturday morning, her family was told she had a couple of hours to live. Her organs were shutting down and her limbs were turning black. She was ninety-five and had lived a long, fruitful life. Suddenly, she sat up and said, "Waffles sound good; let's have some waffles!" She was so radically healed she had waffles and was able to attend the grand reopening the next day. Who can explain this mysterious healing? I am not certain, but I have wondered if God healed her as a prophetic sign that He is going to rip the roof off His church, and He is going to remodel and have signs, wonders, and miracles at the grand re-opening!

How do we create an atmosphere of faith? Here are some ideas:

- Surround yourself with believers, not Christian atheists (they believe in God, but don't believe God) or Christian agnostics (they also believe in God, but are unsure God can do what He says He can do).

- Listen to testimonies or read the testimonies of those who have trusted God and seen miracles. Has your faith level been affected by reading the testimonies in this chapter?

- Pull your prayers into the now. It is tempting to pray in generalities for what we are asking. We also can fall into the trap of not having the faith that God will act now. Sure, we are praying for someone to establish a relationship with the Lord, but we don't have the expectation that they would do so today, but maybe someday. When we pull our prayers into the now, we have the faith that they will be answered before we finish our prayer.

Father God,

Thank you for giving me faith to believe in what You have promised. Help me in my unbelief. I want to contribute to creating an atmosphere of faith. I choose to believe You are working now. I choose to pray for things to happen today. If it doesn't happen today, I will awaken in the morning with new mercies. I will believe every morning that my prayers will be answered today. Now faith is. In Jesus' Name, Amen.

Symptom	Potential Problem	Try this Solution
My prayers are not answered.	No faith in the atmosphere.	Change the atmosphere. Release testimonies.

Chapter 15
Cut the Negative Waves!

The title of this chapter is one of my husband's favorite lines from the movie *Kelly's Heroes*.[1] This 1970 wartime comedy follows a group of WWII American soldiers who went AWOL and robbed a bank behind enemy lines. Throughout the movie, Moriarty, played by Gavin MacLeod, is known for pointing out everything that is wrong or missing and every dreadful thing that could happen. This annoys Sergeant Oddball, played by Donald Sutherland, who continually confronts Moriarty about his negative waves. Two lines from the movie serve our purpose in troubleshooting our prayer life:

1. "There you go again, more negative waves, have a little faith baby, have a little faith!"

2. "Why don't you knock it off with those negative waves? Why don't you say something righteous and hopeful for a change?"

Some of us have been living in a spiritual war zone, and like Moriarty, we have succumbed to the "negative waves." It was not intentional; we haven't always been negative, but sometimes life is overwhelming. Especially if we have gone AWOL in a war zone!

There was a time someone falsely accused me of stirring up trouble at a church. I knew I should forgive, but the enemy inserted a little lie that I grabbed onto. The person who accused me was in the leadership of a church. I believed I didn't need to forgive him, because he should have known better. I see this as an obvious lie now, but in my pain and immaturity, I believed it. Anger took root and turned to bitterness. I began to live from an angry, bitter place and the enemy almost destroyed me. It all began with me choosing negativity over forgiveness.

Negativity leads to hopelessness and many times causes us to give up praying. Negativity is also extremely contagious. Like I shared in the last chapter, we can influence the atmosphere around us. One complaining, negative, bitter person can shift a whole group of people, even if they have gathered to do something good, like pray.

I am serious about the importance of dealing with negativity. We need to remember, "Your words are so powerful that they will kill or give life, and the talkative person will reap the consequences" (Proverbs 18:21 TPT).

Negativity works like a magnet and attracts what I call "The Deadly Ds":

- Discouragement
- Doubt
- Double-mindedness
- Disappointment
- Depression
- Diseased heart (hope deferred)
- Done (The mindset of quitting)
- Despair
- Denial
- Deception

- Death
- Demonic oppression
- Disorder
- Disillusionment
- Dissension
- Defeatism
- Debt
- Debauchery
- Disobedience
- Delay

Some of you are probably thinking, *I kind of see myself in this, but I am still praying with faith for my family or my city.* You may have a divided heart (another Deadly D). We can have great faith in several areas, but there can be a broken place in our hearts where the Deadly Ds live, and it is almost impossible to offer a prayer of faith in that part of our lives. Rest assured, if there is a swamp of the Deadly Ds in one part of your heart, they won't be satisfied to stay confined there. They are looking for ways to take fresh territory.

What do we do to overcome this? Amid your struggles, accentuate the positive things about yourself:

- You desire to pray.
- You, deep down, know God is able.
- You have made a commitment to the Lord, and you want to keep that commitment.
- You are not willing to just go through the motions in your prayer life.
- You still find yourselves muttering prayers under your breath throughout the day.
- You are in covenant with a covenant-keeping God, who loves you dearly.

- God still desires to work with you and through you.

- He has not written Ichabod on your forehead! (Ichabod means, "The glory has departed" from 1 Samuel 4:21-22).

Then take the next step:

1. Recognize when you are speaking negatively. Sometimes it is such a habit, we don't even recognize we are being negative. For me, I visited another church where I felt safe. I didn't have my guard up, and when the pastor preached on anger, I saw myself. It was like the pastor held a mirror up so I could see a true reflection of myself. You may know something is off, but can't determine the issue. Praying Psalm 139:23–24 invites the Lord to give us divine appointments with mirrors that help us see ourselves. He may use sermons, songs, movies, the Word, or other people. He knows what will help us see ourselves. We all have blind spots, and we need help to see what we can't see on our own. "God, I invite your searching gaze into my heart. Examine me through and through; find out everything that may be hidden within me. Put me to the test and sift through all my anxious cares. See if there is any path of pain I'm walking on, and lead me back to your glorious, everlasting way—the path that brings me back to you" (Psalm 139:23–24 TPT).

2. Be honest with the people you normally talk with (spouse, family, friends, co-workers) about your intention to quit speaking negatively about your circumstances, current events, and people around you. Maybe they will join in, and you can hold each other accountable.

3. Ask some tough questions:
   - Am I angry about something?
   - Am I walking in unforgiveness?
   - Is there something in my life that I see as unfair?
   - Am I resentful about something or someone?

- Do I see myself as a victim?
- Am I mad at God?
- Am I entertaining accusations against the goodness of God?

Dana Candler goes deeper, describing how entertaining accusations against God impacts us: "Love grown cold is most often the culmination of fainting faith and hope deferred. Our confidence before God is knit to our beliefs about Him. If we begin to subtly believe He is not as good as we'd thought, because of the collisions of what He's allowed or not allowed in our lives, or if we begin to gradually believe the lurking accusations against His heart—that He is disappointed in us or that His heart is closed toward us—our confidence before Him deteriorates."[2] At times, it is difficult to even admit we are angry at God. God is big enough to take it, and by the way, He already knows.

By acknowledging our anger, we bring it to the light. The enemy loves to work in the darkness, so by bringing it to the light, we speak our truth, then we can speak *the* truth. We can pray, "*God, I am really angry at You, and I don't see Your goodness in this situation, but Lord, You have promised to never leave me or forsake me. You don't just love me with an everlasting love, You are love*" (see Hebrews 13:5, Jeremiah 31:3, 1 John 4:8). I also find it helpful to meditate on Scripture that declares His goodness.

> *We can try all we want to control the negativity coming out of our mouths, but if our hearts are bitter, our speech will show it.*

We can try all we want to control the negativity coming out of our mouths, but if our hearts are bitter, our speech will show it. "For what has been stored up in your hearts will be heard in the overflow of your words" (Matthew 12:34b TPT).

Forgive. Release your anger. Kick out a spirit of anger. Realize life isn't fair. Reaffirm the Lord is able to watch over what isn't fair.

Go to the root of the resentment. "Guard your heart above all else, for it determines the course of your life" (Proverbs. 4:23 NLT).

Dear Lord,

Please forgive me for my negativity and pessimism. I acknowledge it is draining me of faith and affecting my prayer life. I don't want to live with the deadly Ds and I sure don't want the deadly Ds spreading in my life. I am Your beloved son or daughter, and You are for me. "Set a guard over my mouth, LORD; keep watch over the door of my lips" (Psalm 141:3). You are faithful even if I am not. Holy Spirit, help me to see when I am being negative. Lord, I ask You to empower me to be an overcomer. I want to be victorious. I choose to be an overcomer. I choose to speak words of life over my life. In Jesus' Name, Amen.

Symptom	Potential Problem	Try this Solution
My prayers are not answered.	Negativity.	Cut the "negative waves." Be accountable. Ask tough questions to expose the root issue.

Chapter 16
Let Go of Control

Everyone in our church loved the Anderson family. They were beautiful, kind, talented, and anointed. After praying about their next assignment, they believed the Lord was leading them to minister in Europe for a season. My husband and I were at an elders meeting discussing the care of parishioners when we were surprised one elder admitted she was praying the Anderson's move to Europe wouldn't work out. This seasoned intercessor admittedly decided she knew what was best for this family and was praying against the Lord's and the Anderson's will.

One reason our prayers may not be answered by Father God is the motive behind our prayers is not pure. Our selfish and carnal desires can affect what we pray. Our motives may not be blatantly evil, but can be selfish, fearful, or controlling. Prayer is cooperating with the Holy Spirit to see God's power released. When someone is not in agreement with God's plans, their "prayers" can be an attempt to manipulate a different outcome. We are no longer praying from the place of, "Thy will be done" as Jesus instructed us in the model prayer (see Luke 11:1–4).

Satan counterfeits God. He copies. So, if God has us pray out of a place of intimacy with Him and from "Thy will be done" is it not understandable to say that Satan would have us "pray" from the place of "*My* will be done"? When we pray, for whatever reason, to control another person's choices or circumstances, we might be praying prayers that are not pleasing to the Father.

Friends, let's look at this from the perspective of Father God's character. Often, we hear believers say something like, "Well, God is in control." This is frequently said in the midst of a very difficult situation where a person may be innocently declaring they trust God and His work in their lives. On the other hand, it can be a person saying they might as well give up because God is in control. There is not a verse in Scripture that states God is in control. He could be, but He chooses not to be. Many things get blamed on Father God with this questionable theology. God doesn't control traffic, people, or diseases. He can and does intervene in all these things, but to say He is in control implies everything happening is His desire. More accurately we can say He is sovereign, or in other words, that He has supreme power and authority. He is in charge, but he gives us free will so we can *choose* to love and obey Him. He doesn't want robots He controls, but sons and daughters He loves, who choose to honor and love Him.

> *He does not override our wills and we shouldn't pray in such a way that we are trying to control or manipulate others' choices.*

Most people who declare "God is in control" probably mean He is in charge, but when we declare He is in control, it creates many issues for those who have been through horrific experiences. Questions like, "If God is in control, why did he let bad things happen to me?" or countless other questions. If He is controlling all things, why even bother to pray? Satan, on the other hand, wants to control. If we pray to try to control another person, we are aligning with the spirit the enemy operates in, not the way our loving Heavenly Father operates. Remember God rules and Satan controls. Be careful of praying in such a way that your prayers are to control another's will. He does not override our wills and we shouldn't pray in such a way that we are trying to control or manipulate others' choices. We can tap into the Holy Spirit as we pray, or we can tap into another spirit.

For example, we had some young friends who took a new job in a new city. Everything pointed to this move being the will of God. When they moved, they hadn't yet sold their old home. For months, they lived with church members in their new city while waiting for their house to sell. Other houses in their former neighborhood were selling, and they would get interested buyers, but for one reason or another the deal would fall through. As I was praying for them, I sensed someone was praying from a place of their own selfish desires that the house would not sell, requiring this young couple to move back to their former town and job. I didn't discern that these were evil people. They were praying from that distorted place of putting their will and opinions above God's. I asked our friends if they thought that there might be some people who "loved" them, who might be praying that their house wouldn't sell. They looked at each other, got that knowing look on their faces, and they both nodded yes. So, we took authority over every well-meaning but self-willed prayer that could be keeping this house from selling. Within a short period, their house sold, they bought a new home, and they moved forward into their future. I use the word "prayers" in the sense that it is something being said to cause something to change or not change. When we pray from a wrong spirit, our "prayers" at the least may not be answered, but at worst we may be unknowingly empowering the demonic.

Just to restate and make sure we are perfectly clear; our prayer's answer can be delayed because another person's will is involved. It is sometimes difficult to wait, but we need to give God time to work in another person's life the way *He* sees best. In the delay, we can pray for others in many ways, but we must be careful to not cross the line and use the power of prayer or any other spiritual gift to try to control another person's will or to project what we desire onto another person.

If the discussion concerning God being in control vs. God being in charge is new to you, and you desire to learn more. I recommend Harold Eberle's video "God's Involvement With This World[1]."

Dear Lord,

Forgive us for any time we have prayed from the place of "My will be done." Sometimes, out of a place of fear and wanting to help, we have crossed the line. Thank You for loving us and wanting us to freely come to You, to choose to serve You, and obey You. Help me to love like You do. Show us how to pray for those we love without crossing this line. Holy Spirit, I ask You to help me see my motives clearly. Convict me when I pray from a place of fear or control. I choose to submit to God. I choose to resist the devil and he will flee from me (see James 4:7 NKJV). In Jesus' Name, Amen.

Symptom	Potential Problem	Try this Solution
My prayers are not answered.	Praying prayers to try to control another person's choices or circumstances.	Let go of control. Submit to God.

Chapter 17
Mundane Prayers

Mundane isn't a word we often use. According to Dictionary. com, it means "common, ordinary; banal, unimaginative." Its second definition is fascinating: "of or relating to this world or earth as contrasted with heaven."[1] I even had to look up part of the definition because I didn't know *banal* meant "devoid of freshness or originality."[2]

Mundane. At times this is a perfect description of my prayer life. Common, ordinary, related to this world as contrasted with heaven, lacking in freshness or originality. Can you identify with this description?

I was recently asked, as part of a panel discussion, "How do we balance the stuff we must do in the natural world, like keeping house, working a job, paying bills, and taking care of children, with what we want to do in the spiritual realm?" If this isn't the $10,000 question for most Christians, it would at least be in the top five. We all have mundane tasks that we must do. The younger our children, the more dependent they are on the adults in the home to take care of these tasks. These are the common tasks of laundry and dishes, and the ordinary jobs of breaking up fights and paying the bills. These tasks take our time, energy, and focus. As a mother of six children born in an eleven-year span, I understand the common and ordinary. As I looked up the word mundane in the dictionary, I realized part of the key to dealing with the common and ordinary is to not let the rest of the definition apply. Although our days may be common and ordinary, we don't have to allow them to be unimaginative and banal.

Our lives can become mundane, not because we are doing common and ordinary tasks, but because we have become devoid of freshness and originality.

Our lives can become mundane, not because we are doing common and ordinary tasks, but because we have become devoid of freshness and originality. Anything we do regularly can become devoid of freshness and originality. This is true of doing laundry, making love to our spouse, preaching a sermon, or going to coffee with a friend. The problem isn't the activity. Nothing I know of is insulated from the world of the mundane.

Could your prayer life and time in the Word ever be described as mundane? Mine could. The key to living this life well and not being swallowed by the common and ordinary is to keep freshness and originality in our lives.

The more mundane our prayer lives, the less we pray. The less we pray, the fewer prayers we see answered. The fewer prayers we see answered, the easier it is to doubt our prayers' effectiveness. Our prayer life could then be described as a downward spiral.

How do we avoid a mundane life?

- Avoid the rut of doing it the same way every time. Our small church loves to receive communion together, and we have been practicing it more regularly. We found that if my husband and I, the pastors, are the ones who always pray over the elements, we tend to pray very similar prayers. I don't want to say it was mundane, because it is The Lord's Supper and we all value it highly, but when we asked others to pray over the elements, we found a creativity and freshness that infuses our times. Last night, two different women actually sang spontaneously over the elements. It was glorious! So fresh, but also so full of the Word and power. Your tradition might not allow this, so don't get distracted by that, but let it encourage you to ask, "What am I doing the same way every time in my prayer life?"

- Put on joyful music and laugh and dance while doing some daily tasks.

- Focus on the people and not the tasks in your life. Maybe you teach a Bible study; you are teaching people the Bible, not teaching the Bible to people. Another example: you aren't just folding clothes; you are folding your family's clothes. Shift the focus!

- Tap into the well of creativity in a specific area of your life and let the creativity flow into the more common or ordinary areas of your life. Studies have shown if we do something creative, even something simple like coloring a picture, knitting a washcloth, or making a dessert, it will cause creativity to flow more freely in your life.

- Quit comparing. Whether comparing your house, your children, your body, or your prayer life with others, it robs us of confidence and contentment. If we are comparing with others, we can always find someone who is doing worse (comparing from a place of pride), or we can find someone doing better (comparing from a place of insecurity). God isn't concerned about how eloquent our prayers are. At the time of this writing, I have six grandchildren, Moses (8), Luna and Merrigold (5), Juniper and Elvis (3), and little Ocean (2). They all speak with different levels of clarity and eloquence, some can't quite say their Rs. Elvis sounds like he is speaking in tongues most of the time, except when saying the name of an animal. My heart turns to the sound of their voices without any concern on how clearly their request is sent. I hear them from a place of love, just like our Heavenly Father hears us.

- Try reading a different version of the Bible. Try *The Message, The Passion Translation, The Voice,* or *New Living Translation.* (You may want to keep your study Bible for study time, but use one of these versions for your devotional time.)

Most believers don't intentionally turn their back on the Lord, instead it starts with drifting away from Him.

- Most believers don't intentionally turn their back on the Lord, instead it starts with drifting away from Him. "Creeping separateness."[3] We can fall into creeping separateness, but we must make the choice to come back into His presence. We can't fall back into it! Get into the presence of the Lord. As Psalm 16:11 states, "In Your presence is fullness of joy" (NKJV). Joy breaks us out of the mundane. Ask for His refreshing.

- Sometimes it is helpful to "eat out." We normally have our time with the Lord at home. We worship until we sense His presence. We are responsible for hearing from the Lord. There are other times when we need to "eat out" and let someone else create the atmosphere and bring the meal. Just as in the natural realm, it is not healthy to "eat out" all the time. It is also true spiritually, but at times it can give us the boost or realignment we need. This is especially true for leaders who have been giving out a great deal.

- Pray specific prayers and keep track of what you are praying, so that you can see the results of your prayers. Noticing the tangible results infuses excitement into our prayer lives.

Over the years I have kept different types of prayer journals. Some were lists of people I prayed for, while other times I would write out prayers in one color pen and then change pens as I listened for what the Lord said. There were seasons I would grow lax and might only write one or two words down from a whole prayer time. The great thing about journals is you have a record of your walk with the Lord. There is nothing that infuses freshness into your prayers like seeing the Lord's faithfulness to you.

As a young mom, I started a prayer notebook. It was nothing fancy, just a 5x7-inch red spiral notebook in which I would keep a list of people that I prayed for. I had some things I prayed for every day, and then I had other requests divided into different days. Some days I prayed for those who didn't know Jesus, and other days I prayed for extended family or church leadership. I was very diligent to make an X every time I prayed for them. Friends would give me requests that I would list in my little book. A freshness infused my prayer life as I crossed off requests as the Lord answered them. It built my faith. During this time, I had a friend JoAnn, who had a grown daughter who wasn't walking with the Lord. It burdened JoAnn, and she asked me to pray for her. I wrote her in my book as JoAnn's daughter, and I started making my Xs.

We moved on from that town and I moved to a different method during my prayer time, but I kept those prayer journals from that season of my life. We moved many times over a period of about fifteen years. I kept those prayer journals because they were precious to me.

We were now living in Colorado, helping with a small church. One couple that joined the church was such a blessing. They were kind, generous, devoted, and hardworking. They invited us over to their house for dinner one night and we gladly went. As Cindy was finishing up the last-minute details, I was talking to her in her kitchen. On the refrigerator was her collection of cookbooks. I saw an Eastside Baptist Cookbook.

"That's interesting. We went to an Eastside Baptist Church, where is this cookbook from?" I asked.

Cindy responded, as she continued to cook. "Oh, that is from my mom's church in Fort Smith, Arkansas."

I was so surprised, "That was our church! Who is your mom? I wonder if I knew her back then."

"JoAnn Brents"

I couldn't believe my ears; she was the daughter of our good friend who we had lost touch with. We had a wonderful evening enjoying the food and company.

A few days later, I came across a box with some old journals. As I glanced through them, I saw my old faded red journal where I started keeping track of my prayers. I turned the pages slowly. As I read the list of those who didn't know Jesus, I saw,

"JoAnn's daughter: XXXXXXXXXXXXXXXXXXXXXXXXXX XXXXX"

What an infusion of joy hit my prayer life! I had not remembered praying for her. I realized my loving Father had answered that prayer in an incredible way and allowed me the joy of being her friend.

Father God,

Thank you for hearing and responding from the place of love. Show me where I have drifted away and allowed my prayers to be mundane. Breathe fresh life and faith into my prayer life. I receive your invitation to me.

"You must catch the troubling foxes,
those sly little foxes that hinder our relationship.
For they raid our budding vineyard of love
to ruin what I've planted within you.
Will you catch them and remove them for me?
We will do it together*" (Song of Songs 2:15 TPT).*

I receive this invitation and am thankful for this life we live together.

I acknowledge that You, oh Lord, are the Lover of my soul, the Creator of the universe, the Father who loves and adores me, and yet I have let our conversation and time together become mundane. Forgive me. I acknowledge that as it has become mundane, I have let creeping separateness come into our relationship. I want to fall in love with You all over again. I want to partner with You. Give me a hunger for Your Word. Let my glances turn into gazes. I speak freshness into the ordinary. Surprise me! Encounter me! Open my eyes and refresh my spirit. Thank you for inviting me into the process of catching the little foxes that hinder our relationship. In Jesus' Name, Amen.

Symptom	Potential Problem	Try this Solution
My prayers are not answered.	Mundane praying.	Seek freshness. Do something different. Keep track of your prayers and the answers.

Chapter 18
Tug of War

I was a little uncomfortable in the large gathering of women. I had been a follower of Jesus for twenty years, but this gathering catered to women from a different neighborhood of the body of Christ. These women were much more vocal and active than I was accustomed to. There were women dancing and kneeling and waving flags and raising their hands. It wasn't that I didn't think they were authentic in their faith and genuine in their love for God; it was just *so* different.

Cindy Jacobs, a minister and prophet with a global reputation for her prayer movements, healing gift, and prophetic ministry, ministered by calling up people in need of healing. I had plantar fasciitis, which caused me a great deal of pain. I had read a book Cindy had written, and I trusted her, so I decided to go forward. Before too long she declared, "Someone has pain in their right heel, and God is healing it right now." Instantly, my right heel was pain-free, and I was healed! Nothing like this had ever happened to me. I was so excited and grateful, but also a little confused. If He was going to heal my right heel, why not heal the left one as well?

Fast forward several months. Jack and I attended the Light the Nation conference in Dallas. We were hungry for all God had for us, but again, it was a little awkward for us. We were up on the balcony on the first night because it seemed a little safer there. We could see what was going on, but we felt more like spectators than participants. Again, Cindy Jacobs was ministering and calling out ailments God was healing. My right heel felt wonderful ever since the women's conference, but my left heel was in a lot of pain. Before I knew it, she had everyone who was having pain in their left heel stand. I stood up with great faith and excitement. He had healed my right foot; He could do the same for my left. I by faith received my healing. Again, the pain left, and I saw my life changing. No more pain!

> *Many who haven't seen their prayers answered are using the right strategy, praying with the right heart, but just have not finished the task.*

After the meeting was over, we went back to the hotel. As we were walking back, I felt a little pain in my left heel. I steadfastly declared, "No! I do not receive that pain; my heel has been healed!" Over the next six weeks, I had to fight for the healing of my left foot.

Any time I would feel pain, I would declare no to the pain because God had healed my foot. The symptoms of pain came less and less often until my foot was completely healed. I believe the Lord was teaching me an important lesson. If I had embraced the pain and called it "my plantar fasciitis," I think I would have lost the healing God was desiring to give me. Instead, I learned that many times, we need to continually fight for the answer to our prayer.

As in boxing, sometimes the hit will knock the enemy unconscious, and the fight is over. But other times, after the first blow, a tug of war ensues, and the key is to not let go of the rope. We pray and see some breakthrough in our health situation, a relationship, our finances, or in the government, and we relax and quit praying as diligently, or quit praying at all, and the next thing we know there has been a counter-tug that pulls us off balance.

Many who haven't seen their prayers answered are using the right strategy, praying with the right heart, but just have not finished the task. "One day Jesus taught the apostles to keep praying and never stop or lose hope" (Luke 18:1 TPT). Our focus in prayer must be the Lord. We can't get discouraged and stop when we don't see changes, and we shouldn't rejoice and stop praying until the Lord shows us it is finished. He might do this by lifting the burden to pray or a peace settles on us as we pray. There is no formula for this; we just have to develop the ability to connect with the Lord and let Him guide us. We can't let circumstances sway our prayers. Even when a person we are praying for finishes a task, gets saved, or is healed, our prayer assignment might not be finished. We have all seen new believers who turn away, people who have experienced a relapse after being healed, or someone who faces a challenge after completing an important task. It raises the question of whether someone abandoned their intercession too soon. We can't take away the mystery of why some prayers are unanswered or some people aren't healed, but we can walk closely with the Lord so we know we have done our part.

Dutch Sheets, in his book *Intercessory Prayer*, shares the story of being asked by a woman to visit her sister and pray for her healing. The woman didn't give him the whole story, because she was scared he wouldn't go. The doctors didn't give the sister, who he calls Diane, much hope of living. She was in a coma, and the doctors didn't expect her to come out of the coma. But if she did, she would have extensive brain damage, limiting her ability to function. Dutch went sixty or seventy times to pray for this young woman, praying an hour or more each time.

Dutch explains, "It didn't work out as expected. Life rarely does, does it? I expected the Lord to heal this young lady through our prayers in a dramatic, easy, quick way. After all, that's how it happened with Jesus.

- I didn't expect to invest three to four hours of my life each week for a year (including travel time).

- I didn't expect humiliation and insults from the staff of the nursing home where she stayed.

- I didn't expect to cry so much.
- I didn't expect to be so bold at times.
- I didn't expect to be so intimidated at times.
- I didn't expect it to take so long.
- I didn't expect to learn so much!"[1]

God completely restored Diane on a Saturday morning when she was by herself.

What if Dutch would have decided whether he was going to be successful in his prayers based on what he saw with his natural eyes? He explained that he wasn't just hopeful she would be healed but had great faith she would be healed. Many of those who describe praying for miracles or salvations speak of stepping into a place of great faith, not because of what they see with their eyes, but based on what the Lord was doing in their own hearts.

Dutch goes on to say, "A lack of endurance is one the greatest causes of defeat, especially in prayer."[2]

There are times the battle in prayer feels like a tug of war. We sense a great surge where victory feels at hand and the next thing we know, the tug in the other direction is so hard we almost fall on our faces. We can't underestimate the effectiveness of our prayers. Hang on to the rope! Persevere! Ask for faith to stand. "Remember to stay alert and hold firmly to all that you believe. Be mighty and full of courage" (1 Corinthians 16:13 TPT).

Dear Lord,

My desire is to be a finisher! But so many times I waver based on what I am seeing. Help me to be so in tune with You that I see things from Your perspective. Help me to not be deterred from my prayer assignment by what seems like victories or defeats. Lord, let me receive my daily prayer assignments from You. Let me live and pray from a place of faithfulness. I choose to stand firm. In Jesus' Name, Amen.

Symptom	Potential Problem	Try this Solution
My prayers are not answered.	Giving up too soon. Forgetting to be persistent.	Be alert. Finish the assignment.

Chapter 19
Lonely Prayers

Again I tell you, if two of you on earth agree (harmonize together, make
a symphony together) about whatever [anything and everything] they may
ask, it will come to pass and be done for them by My Father in heaven
(Matthew 18:19 AMPC).

In the Gospel of Matthew, Jesus emphasizes the importance of
agreement. In contrast, in the book of John, Jesus says, "If you ask
Me anything in My name, I will do it" (John 14:14 NASB). Thayer's Greek Lexicon explains that "ask" means, "ask for one's self."[1]

We all hear things from our own perspective. John, the beloved
disciple, was in Jesus' inner circle and was often referred to in a
group. He tells us to ask for ourselves. In contrast, Matthew, who
was a hated tax-collector before he came to Christ, tells us to get
agreement. Both are quoting Jesus. Remember, there was no way to
electronically record what Jesus said. They wrote from their mem-
ory. Maybe John usually prayed in a group while Matthew prayed
alone. Perhaps when Jesus taught the disciples how to pray, the
teaching they remembered was to pray in a way that they normally
didn't. John, who was in the inner circle, needed to remind himself
and others to pray individually. Matthew, who in many ways was
an outcast, had to remind himself to get others to agree with him
in prayer.

It is true God will answer our individual prayers, but there is also power in agreement.

It is true God will answer our individual prayers, but there is also power in agreement that is alluded to in Matthew's Gospel. We all know people who have experienced being hurt by the church or a prayer group. Before too long they become isolated, and they pray from that lonely place. We all should spend part of our prayer time alone. But if all our times of prayer are spent in isolation, this can be dangerous. Dangerous? Really? Sadly, I have seen it to be true.

Remember how Elijah thought he was the only one left and became despondent? When? After a huge confrontation, when he was exhausted, isolated, and alone (see 1 Kings 18:16–19:18). In reality, there were seven thousand men who hadn't bowed their knees to Baal in Israel. I have seen friends who also were isolated and heard the enemy and attributed it to God. Shortly thereafter, these friends were not doing well and were in a place of great confusion. If we are not careful, we can pray from a place of hurt.

Instead, if we pray with others, there is the power of agreement and also the safety of accountability. Notice Matthew 18:19 speaks of harmonizing and a symphony. Praying in agreement does not mean that you will say the same thing as those praying with you. Harmony needs different sounds. A symphony implies there are many different sounds which complement each other. I find that with my gift mix, praying with others who have different gifts is helpful. Mercy is not my first response to situations, so when I pray with merciful people, it brings harmony to my prayers. We form a symphony when we each follow the Holy Spirit, our conductor, and hear His voice and release our sound. Have you been in groups where they all pray like the leader prays? Where is the symphony?

We all need to find a group to pray with. It might be weekly with your best friend over the phone, or it could be a group of young mothers that gather at the park to pray and watch their kids play. Perhaps you and your spouse or another family member can find time to pray together. Coworkers may be able to meet together over lunch. It could be several guys meeting on their way home from work once a week. If you have not seen your prayers answered, is it because you have been lacking agreement? This is especially important for the single adult!

Our friend and church member, Cynthia, was having a difficult time at work. She had worshiped and warred over the situation. She had asked others to pray for her, but then one Saturday night, as our church gathered, we all got in agreement with her. We listened to the Holy Spirit and in agreement prayed fully over her situation. Within twelve hours they moved her boss out of his position, and things shifted in her work assignment.

"Again I say to you, that if two of you agree on earth about anything that they may ask, it shall be done for them by My Father who is in heaven" (Matthew 18:19 NASB). We tend to read past familiar verses like Matthew 18:19, but these verses are actual keys that we need in our prayer life.

Often, when we share prayer requests, we say, "Pray that . . ." and we tell the person what to pray. Remember, Matthew 18:19 speaks of harmony and symphony. If someone prays exactly what you tell them to pray, are we getting the harmony we need? The key is to pray together over a situation or person causing different perspectives and sounds to come forth. This creates the harmony. When we are praying about something that we are passionate about, we can get tunnel vision. Getting prayers of agreement can broaden our perspective.

Many years ago, I received a prayer request to pray for my friend's niece. There were people all over our region praying for this little girl, who kept getting sicker and sicker. Some were from her school and church while others were friends of her family. Still others were her aunt's friends. None of us were in the same room. We were praying in agreement even though we weren't physically together. I didn't spend hours praying for this little girl, although I am sure some of the people did. As I began to pray, my thoughts went to the doctor, and I prayed that he would quit focusing on the same issue but would look at her sickness from a new perspective. As I recall, this was about all I prayed for her. Later, I heard that the little girl was doing better, and indeed the doctor had looked at things from a different perspective and had seen something he hadn't seen before. This helped her get better and eventually fully recover. Did my prayers cause her to be healed? No, they were just part of the symphony. I was like the person who plays the triangle in the orchestra. I just rang it once or twice, while others played (prayed) for hours, and together, in our agreement, we saw our prayers answered and an extremely sick little girl recover.

There is a synergy that comes from praying with others. Draft horses give us a beautiful picture of synergy. Dave Ramsey, in his book EntreLeadership wrote,

> One of the largest, strongest horses in the world is the Belgian draft horse. Competitions are held to see which horse can pull the most and one Belgian can pull 8,000 pounds. The weird thing is if you put two Belgian horses in the harness who are strangers to each other, together they can pull 20,000–24,000 pounds. Two can pull not twice as much as one but three times as much as one. This example represents the power of synergy. However, if the two horses are raised and trained together, they learn to pull and think as one. The trained, and therefore unified, pair can pull 30,000–32,000 pounds, almost four times as much as a single horse.[2]

I have seen this work in prayer times. As I pray alone, I at times have sensed a flow and seen things move, or in other words, seen results. Also, I can pray with strangers and sometimes we hit a place of agreement, and we see things move. But the times I have felt most effective in my prayers are when I have prayed regularly with the same group of women. The Holy Spirit trained us in prayer together and we saw answers to our prayers. A flow and an ease came as we learned to trust each other and work together to see results.

One group I was involved with prayed together every Tuesday for years. We prayed for one leader in the morning, had lunch together, and then prayed in the afternoon for a different leader. Although we normally prayed for these leaders, neither of them wanted to constrain us if the Lord wanted us praying for something else. There was an ease and a power that came from being trained in the yoke together. We learned to defer to each other's strengths and cover each other's weaknesses. We loved each other and prayed for each other's families, which made each of us stronger individually.

You might say, "Well goody for you, I don't have a group of people like that." True, but maybe you can. When this Tuesday group stopped because people moved, I had a choice to isolate or to look for new places to connect. It didn't happen immediately, but I now have two groups I pray with regularly.

Pray for people to pray with and open your eyes. Be willing to make new friends. Be willing to try praying with them and be diligent to persevere. Anytime we are in a place of intimacy in prayer, we will see things in others that aren't perfect. Remember that they are seeing imperfections in you as well! Extend grace to each other. This doesn't work if you wear a mask and hide from the others, only letting the good show. Transparency is required.

We can work synergistically with our friends, fellow church members, or a fellow intercessor, but also with the prayers of those in history. "Not one of these people, even though their lives of faith were exemplary, got their hands on what was promised. God had a better plan for us: that their faith and our faith would come together to make one completed whole, their lives of faith not complete apart from ours" (Hebrews 11:39–40 MSG). We are not communicating with the dead, but the Word says the prayers of the saints are in bowls in heaven. Bowls are meant for mixing. If prayers needed to be kept separate, wouldn't the Lord have told us that our prayers are in files in heaven? Our prayer can agree with biblical prayers or prayers of our country's founders or religious leaders who are now in heaven.

The Word tells us also that none of Samuel's words fell to the ground. This statement implies some words or prayers could fall to the ground, but Samuel's didn't. Where did they go? They are alive and active, and our prayers can synergize with them. Scripture seems to show us that our prayers are effective when we pray by ourselves (John 14:14, James 5:16), but also states that there is power in agreement.

Dear Lord,

Thank You for giving us keys to aid us in our prayer life. Help us to not only carry the keys, but to know what each is for and how to use each one. I thank You for those I can agree with in prayer and create the symphony and harmony You desire. Lord, I lift up those who are praying alone and are isolated. Lord, I ask that You help them to see who they could pray with. Give them a hunger to believe for others with whom they can make a symphonic sound. We break isolation off them, and we thank You for the accountability of praying with one another. We want to first agree with You in our prayers; help us to agree with Your heart and with Your prayers. Let us be wise in what we pray. Lord, if there are things held up needing our agreement, show us. In Jesus' Name, Amen.

Symptom	Potential Problem	Try this Solution
My prayers are not answered.	Lonely prayers. Prayers lacking agreement.	Find a prayer partner or group.

Chapter 20
No Action

"We never know how God will answer our prayers, but we can expect that He will get us involved in His plan for the answer. If we are true intercessors, we must be ready to take part in God's work on behalf of the people for whom we pray." – Corrie ten Boom [1]

Whether on the playground or in the prayer room, talk is cheap. It is easy to let an abundance of words flow. But are we willing to invest in what we are praying about? Are we willing to do the dirty work? Are we willing to invest our time in people? I have heard several pastors joke, "Pastoring would be easy if it weren't for the people." As we prepared to teach Vacation Bible School in the 1990s, I remember our friend Bonnie Robinson wisely stating, "Remember, you are not teaching the Bible to children, you are teaching children the Bible." It is about our focus being on the children, not just the facts of the Bible story we plan to share. We are doing our best to connect people with the God who loves them. He has the answer to their every need.

Each of us has been bestowed with a divine calling from God, encompassing a specific assignment that often aligns with our deepest passions. We need to exercise caution and not presume everyone shares our same purpose. We are to actively engage and dedicate ourselves to our unique calling, but it is not a calling intended for everyone. If you are called to overturn abortion, that is important. All of us should be pro-life, but it might look different for the person who is called to care for the young mothers versus those who are called to pray at abortion clinics. If you are called to care for the poor, you will spend your time differently than an intercessor. You should pray, and the intercessor should have a concern for the poor, but how each spends their time and resources will vary. Don't judge others and don't expect them to see life exactly the way you do through the glasses you wear.

> *Part of praying for a situation is making ourselves available to be an answer to our own prayer.*

God gives us the passion to pray about a certain situation. We diligently pray over it without recognizing that God is waiting on us to be part of the answer to our prayers. We can become content to pray without being involved personally in the answer to the prayer or even seeing answers to our prayers. Contentment is good, but not if we become content to not impact the world around us. We must position ourselves to hear the Lord, pray with all the faith we can muster, and then live, willing to take the risks needed to impact this broken and hurting world. We may pray for elections, but we also need to vote. We can pray for the poor, but we need to look for opportunities to give to and serve the poor as well. As James says in James 1:22 (MSG), "Don't fool yourself into thinking that you are a listener when you are anything but, letting the Word go in one ear and out the other. Act on what you hear!"

Part of praying for a situation is making ourselves available to be an answer to our own prayer. Another aspect of praying is continuing to pray through until we sense from the Holy Spirit that we have been heard. Arthur Wallis, a Christian author and teacher known for his works on prayer and spiritual revival, explains, "Praying through includes praying ourselves through to the place where we are ready to do whatever God may require of us."[2]

The Bible has many examples of people praying over a situation and consequently being part of the solution. Nehemiah, after hearing a troubling report concerning Jerusalem, explained, "When I heard this, I sat down and wept. In fact, for days I mourned, fasted, and prayed to the God of heaven" (Nehemiah 1:4 NLT). His great concern for Jerusalem showed on his countenance such that the king noticed. "The king asked, 'Well, how can I help you?' With a prayer to the God of heaven, I replied, 'If it pleases the king, and if you are pleased with me, your servant, send me to Judah to rebuild the city where my ancestors are buried'" (Nehemiah 2:4–5 NLT). Nehemiah was bold in his prayers to God. Still, he also had to take action and make a request of the king to boldly lead the rebuilding of the wall around Jerusalem. It was a dangerous and difficult task, which required him to deal with dissension and complexities even amongst those committed to helping with the restoration.

Jesus, teaching the disciples in Matthew 9:37–38, encouraged them to pray for God to send workers out into the harvest. Then, in the very next verses in Matthew 10, Jesus gives them the opportunity to answer their prayers, by calling the twelve together and giving them authority to cast out evil spirits and to heal the sick. Immediately He sent them out into the harvest field.

Moses, raised in Pharaoh's house, had great concern for his own people. As a young man, in his zeal to defend his people, he murdered an Egyptian. When he ran for his life, he fled to the land of Midian for forty years. The Bible doesn't mention it, but I imagine he prayed many prayers for the Israelites' deliverance from the Egyptians. Yet Moses was shocked when God told him that He planned to use him to bring deliverance to his people. He responded with a great deal of "what ifs" and "buts" (see Exodus 3:1– 4, 17). Part of his dilemma may have been his own insecurities, but he also may not have wanted to get involved after failing the last time. Maybe he had gotten comfortable and saw the stronghold of Israel's slavery as unchangeable. When facing what appears to be unchangeable circumstances, or a situation where we have failed in the past, we often find it easier to pray about the situation than to step into the predicament, even at the Lord's prompting. Just as Corrie Ten Boom said in the opening quote to this chapter, we must be ready to take part in God's work.

Not only in Biblical times, but throughout history, God calls on many to be involved in the answer to their own prayers. The story of Sophie Scholl has deeply challenged me: at just twenty-one years old, she played a crucial role in the student resistance movement against the Nazis known as The White Rose Society. Alongside her older brother Hans, Sophie fearlessly distributed leaflets and used graffiti to denounce the Nazi regime, calling for resistance against its crimes and the ongoing war, even when much of the German church remained silent as Hitler killed approximately six million Jews and the war ravaged much of Europe and Russia. Surely, Christians prayed, but there are times when we must stand in the face of evil. Despite the danger, Sophie and her fellow members of The White Rose Society stood up against the Nazi wickedness, ultimately facing execution for what the Nazis declared were acts of treason. In her final moments, she declared, "How can we expect righteousness to prevail when there is hardly anyone willing to give herself up individually to a righteous cause? Such a fine sunny day, and I have to go, but what does death matter, if through us thousands of people are awakened and stirred to action?"[3] What amazing courage to take action, even in the face of such evil.

Father God,

I want to actively partner with You. I am looking earnestly for answers to my prayers and for ways to do my part in what I am praying about. I don't want to get into striving and thinking everything is my responsibility, but I think there is a bigger danger for me to passively wait when You are asking me to act. Help me to hear You clearly and respond quickly. In Jesus' Name, Amen.

Symptom	Potential Problem	Try this Solution
My prayers are not answered.	Praying without action	You may be part of the answer to what you are praying. Is God waiting on you to do something?

Chapter 21
Seeking His Hand

Elvis is our fifth grandchild. His parents picked his name long before he was born on Elvis Presley's birthday. He has red hair, brown eyes, and a bigger-than-life personality. His parents went through a difficult time from the time he was two to four years old. As can easily happen, his parents got used to buying him toys every time they went to the store. Nothing extravagant, but it built an expectation.

One time when Elvis found out I was going to Target, he immediately started naming all the toys he wanted. "They have Legos, trucks, and dinosaurs and . . ." As a seasoned mom and grandma, I ignored all of this, focusing on getting out of the house.

I returned in about an hour, forgetting Elvis had given me a shopping list. He excitedly came to meet me as he heard the front door open. He didn't speak to me or hug me or really even notice me. All he wanted to do was search the red and white bags that I carried in the door. He became more intense and agitated as he searched from bag to bag, finding nothing he had listed off. In exasperation, he put his hands on his hips and declared, "There are toys at Target! You just have to go look in the right aisles!" He couldn't fathom that I could know there were toys in the store, yet I didn't get him anything. I must be ignorant of the fact that there are toys in the store.

If we are not careful, we will have expectations without relationship.

As new believers, it is so exciting to see our prayers answered. Our faith grows. Our love for God grows. If we are not careful, we will become like Elvis and have expectations without relationship. Father God wants to answer our prayers, but He loves us and wants to have a relationship with us. He wants to spend time with us. Even in fasting, when we are seeking a breakthrough, we can fix our eyes on the answer we want. We focus on the breakthrough needed and pray for God to move. Maybe we appear like Elvis to our Heavenly Father. Perhaps He is trying to teach us He is the Giver of all good gifts. Father God may desire us to sit in His presence, gaze at Him, and listen to what is on His heart. God loves us and desires to spend time with us. "Lord when you said to me 'Seek my face;' my inner being responded, 'I'm seeking your face with all my heart'" (Psalm 27:8 TPT).

When I am tempted to make my prayers sound like a six-year-old's Christmas wish list, it helps me to pause and focus on who God is. I have made a list of His wonderful attributes in the back of my Bible. It helps me to pause, focus on who He is, and praise Him. For He is loving, glorious, full of justice and mercy, kind, and patient. It helps to focus on His awesome characteristics instead of what I want.

Father God,

Forgive me, Lord, for focusing on what You can give me and how You can solve my problems. I desire to seek Your heart, not just Your hand. I know You desire to help me, but I also know You don't want me focusing on what You can give me without spending time with You and enjoying You, and loving You. Give me the desire and grace to sit in Your presence. In Jesus' Name, Amen.

Symptom	Potential Problem	Try this Solution
My prayers are not answered.	Seeking the blessings of God without seeking God the Father.	Spend time focusing on the face of God instead of what you desire for Him to give you.

Chapter 22
Doubting ME

One hundred percent of a certain type of prayer goes unanswered. Those are the prayers we don't pray because we doubt God can use us.

In the early 2000s, I took a Wagner Leadership Institute class led by Cindy Jacobs. She told us many stories of God using her in mighty ways all over the world, and she challenged us to believe God could and would use us as well. On the last day of the class, and as was the custom, Cindy prayed a prayer of impartation for each of the students, including me (see 1 Timothy 4:14). I asked the Lord, with great faith, that He would let me receive all He wanted me to have. That evening, around the dinner table, my husband told me about a friend of ours who was hospitalized and scheduled for surgery the next morning because of a twisted bowel. I exclaimed, "I haven't had time to lose the anointing yet. Let's go pray for her. She'll get healed!" My declaration showed I had great faith in God and considerable respect for Cindy's spiritual abilities, but not so much in my own anointing! Jack and I went to the hospital and explained to her that we had great faith for her healing. At the time, we attended a church that didn't talk much about healing. She grew up in a denomination with very little

> *One hundred percent of a certain type of prayer goes unanswered. Those are the prayers we don't pray because we doubt God can use us.*

talk of supernatural healings, yet she extended her faith and agreed with our faith, and she was miraculously healed. No surgery for her! Often, we don't doubt His ability, just our ability to be a conduit to such miraculous power.

We may have great faith in our amazing God. We know He is able to save, heal, deliver, set free, cause breakthroughs, and so much more. We have great faith God will use other people to do these things. We might even enjoy praying for those who minister to others. The danger is that we can put the one ministering on a pedestal and assume that, although not perfect; they are more righteous than us, pray more than us, are more devoted than us, are purer than us, and a multitude of other things that can separate them from us. When a problem arises where we need the faith to access that power for ourselves or see this power flow through us to touch others, we tend to over-evaluate ourselves and the situation. We see our own shortcomings and failures, and we tend to think, "Surely God couldn't use a broken person like me." The longer we evaluate ourselves, the less faith we can muster, but maybe we just need to respond quickly with child-like faith.

For many years, Jack and I lived by faith (which can be synonymous with barely getting by-although it shouldn't be) while raising six children. We prayed in much of our provision, including cars. We drove these cars until they didn't have much life left in them. When our son Luke was nine years old, our car wouldn't start. Jack tried everything he knew to do, but it still wouldn't start. We were all lingering in the front yard deciding what to do when Luke ran over to the car and threw himself over the hood of the car with his arms crossed. He exclaimed, "Be healed in Jesus' name!" We glanced at each other with raised eyebrows and decided we might as well get in agreement with his child-like faith. Jack got in the car, turned the key, and it started right up! My guess is that Luke really wanted to go wherever we were headed, and he just reacted, without really evaluating his anointing, his prayer life, and whether he had read his

Bible that day. There is a time for introspection and a time for bold faith, and we need to know the difference.

When you are spending time with the Lord, it is the ideal time to ask Him to search your heart. Let the Holy Spirit show you what needs to be corrected and what attitudes and behaviors require repentance. As you leave your prayer closet wearing your armor described in Ephesians 6:13–17, be confident that you are in right standing with the Lord. You can then be as bold as a lion, praying with full confidence for everyone and every situation you encounter.

We might conclude God is able to do amazing things but assume He would choose a worthier conduit. But 2 Corinthians 4:7 tells us, "We are like common clay jars that carry this glorious treasure within, so that the immeasurable power will be seen as God's, not ours" (TPT). God uses jars of clay, which were jars used for common, ordinary, daily use. That is us: common, ordinary, but connected to an extraordinary God. He wants us all to carry His glory.

Over the years, I have had the privilege of traveling with several well-known ministers, sometimes in groups and sometimes alone. None of these people are perfect, so we need to get that excuse out of our mind. What they are is diligent, faithful, focused, loving, and aware that God wants to and does use them. More importantly, they have sacrificially made themselves available to the Lord. These are all things we can grow in, so God can use us more often and we can see our prayers answered more regularly.

Dear Lord,

Please forgive me for any way I am hindering You from working through me to do the miraculous or impact others through my prayers. I realize my focus is not on You, but on me. I repent for comparing myself with others. Lord, if You can speak through a donkey, surely You can work through me (see Numbers 22:28). In Jesus' Name, Amen.

Symptom	Potential Problem	Try this Solution
My prayers are not answered.	Doubting God's ability to use someone like me.	Realize God uses ordinary clay jars.

Chapter 23

Becoming a Funnel

Jack had just graduated from seminary, and we were excited to move to a new season of life with baby number five on the way. Our youngest child was three-and-a-half, and we were excited to be re-entering the baby world. Jack went with me for the first ultrasound so he could see our little baby. As the technician performed the ultrasound, she went from very chatty to conspicuously quiet. This was not our first rodeo; we had had six ultrasounds (thanks to our first children being twins) and knew what to expect. But this time she seemed to be taking much longer than usual. She kept going over the same area. Finally, we asked her what was going on. The ultrasound technician showed us her concerns on the screen. She called it "double bubble," and showed us how the stomach was not connected to the intestines. I am not sure she was supposed to show us this, but I am thankful she did.

After the ultrasound, we sat in the waiting room to wait to talk to the doctor. It was so awkward. We were very concerned and didn't know what it meant. My emotions felt so raw, and I wanted a place to hide in the midst of all the pregnant women. Finally, we were called back to talk to a doctor we had never seen before. He, in what could best be called an emotionless monologue, told us of the scenarios we were looking at. Best case scenario is this child has Down syndrome. But it could be another genetic issue, and the worst-case scenario is this child does fine in the womb, but as soon as they are born, they die. We walked out of the office in an emotional stupor. Jack erupted into tears as soon as we got to the parking lot, and I shut down all emotions. As we got in the car, Jack quoted a verse that was on a plaque we had just received from our friends Randy and Kristi as a graduation gift. "'For I know the plans I have for you,' declares the LORD, 'plans to prosper you and not to harm you, plans to give you hope and a future'" (Jeremiah 29:11). It wasn't a verse we were familiar with, but we grabbed ahold of it with all we had.

Jack, who was an associate pastor, had responsibilities at the church that evening. He went to the senior pastor's home and shared our circumstances. The news traveled fast amongst our church friends, and many prayed for us and for our baby.

The next day, I underwent additional tests with more sensitive equipment. After reviewing the results of those tests, the doctor wanted to perform even more tests. We asked if there was anything that could be done for the baby while still in the womb. He replied, "No." So we politely declined further testing. He angrily responded, "You wouldn't be the first Baptist pastor we scheduled an abortion for. You don't know what you are going to do until the grenade lands in your own fox hole." Again, we were left shaken and shocked by the whole thing.

After much prayer by ourselves and others, we had one more ultrasound three months later, which showed no problems with the baby.

When I went into labor, we headed to the hospital and met the emotionless doctor, who we had not seen since his monologue. He motioned to Jack to slip out into the hallway with him. With his face pale, he asked Jack if there had been any changes in the situation since he had last seen us. Jack told him about the good ultrasound. He relaxed.

Luke Jeremiah was born completely healthy at 8 pounds, 2 ounces. We knew the Lord had touched him. The bigger miracle was probably that I was at total peace throughout the pregnancy. I worried less during that pregnancy than any other.

We have seen other miraculous healings in our family and for those we have prayed for, but we have prayed and prayed for many others who haven't been healed. Why? I don't have the answer for that. While I was writing this book, our son Caleb and his wife, Lydia, called to tell us they were expecting again. Their daughters, Merrigold and Juniper, were seven and five at the time. We were all excited for this new addition. A boy! When Lydia was five months along, we got *the* call. Lydia had received an ultrasound and there seemed to be a serious problem with his brain development. They offered to schedule a procedure for the next morning. Lydia, after thinking how kind the woman was acting, realized they were offering to schedule an abortion for their precious baby.

Caleb and Lydia had both given years of their life to pray at the Supreme Court for the ending of abortion. They value life, all life. This was a very challenging call to receive, but we had dealt with this before with our son Luke. I went into the mindset of "*We have faced this battle before. God healed a problem in the womb before, he could and would do it again.*" Faith mode is a great place, unless we enter it with denial or presumption. Faith doesn't deny the problem exists. With faith, we acknowledge the facts about a situation, but we believe the truth of who the Lord is and what He is saying. For example, I might be sick, but I declare the truth that the Lord is a Healer. In denial, we don't even acknowledge the facts or ask the Lord what He has to say about a situation. Our responsibility and intent is to hear the Lord about what he desires to do, and then get in agreement with Him, so our faith lines up with His will.

But when we enter faith mode based on what we desire, or on what God did last time, this is not faith, but presumption. Presumption is defined in Webster's 1828 dictionary as "blind or headstrong confidence, unreasonable confidence in divine favor."[1] Dictionary. com defines it as "to take for granted, assume or suppose."[2]

Remember when David was king and battling enemies, he would inquire of the Lord. In 1 Samuel 23, he inquired of the Lord four times. He would ask the Lord if this was his battle, if he should go into the battle now, and what strategy he should employ. Each new battle required new insight from the Lord. This takes time and discipline. When in a battle, we can choose to default to faith or fear. I would prefer faith. But, when we extend our faith, choosing to stand firm or enter a battle without first inquiring of the Lord, we can fall into the temptation of battling for *our* will, especially when praying for those we love. Because David chose to inquire of the Lord each time, he stayed out of presumption, which is a door to defeat, despair, disappointment, and hope deferred.

When we received the bad report concerning our son Luke, we immediately heard a verse from the Lord. We knew what the Lord said about our situation, and we had faith that God was going to heal our baby or give us the grace needed to handle the challenge. With our grandchild, I entered immediately into a mindset where I presumed to know what God planned to do in this new battle because it was similar to a battle I had seen before. Unlike David, I didn't stop to inquire of the Lord; I stepped into presumption.

Lydia bravely carried little Archie to full term. She and Caleb believed in the best and also looked at the facts about his life with sobriety. I, myself, just remained in "faith" without even acknowledging what might happen. Little Archie lived for two short hours. Even in those two hours, he was a blessing to those who loved him. As I struggled with the trauma and shock of the death of our grandson, who I thought for sure the Lord was going to heal, the Lord showed me I had stepped into presumption. When we enter battles in presumption, we assume we know what God is going to do, this may open a door for the enemy to do us harm, just like if we entered a natural battlefield while assuming we knew how to win with blind confidence.

Here is what I know: Jesus is still in the business of healing. He uses all types of people's prayers. There is not a formula we can follow to guarantee healing, but there are principles that help.

If the only time you know of people being healed is stories from the Bible, it might be helpful to read stories of modern-day healings. Talk to people who have seen healings. Visit a church where healings occur regularly. This may move your faith from "God can heal" to "God does heal."

Often, we decide what we believe by having it line up with *our* experiences. For example, suppose I am not seeing any healings in my church. I might teach that God doesn't do miraculous healings anymore. We also may need to re-evaluate what we believe if our theology is "God sends sickness to teach me things, so I need to embrace my sickness." When we embrace our sickness like this it becomes part of our identity, not something we are battling. Obviously, we can learn things in a time of sickness, but this sickness is not part of who I am. As the saying goes, "The fire the enemy sends to destroy us, God uses to refine us." Out of this theology that God gives sickness, many people embrace their sickness calling it "*my* diabetes" or "*my* heart trouble." I have seen several people show signs of being miraculously healed, but because their identity was so entwined with the sickness, the illness came back just as strong. They were unable to sustain the healing because their identity was in their illness.

Many people and churches struggle deeply when they have fasted and prayed fervently for someone to be healed, and the person dies or continues to suffer. "Healing comes, not because it is deserved, not because a certain formula is used, not because of anyone's 'power or godliness' (Acts 3:12), but because the Spirit is working."[3] Our pastor at Northern Hills Baptist Church, Richard

Hubbard, led our church into a season of many healings. The season began as we fasted and prayed for a matriarch in the church who eventually died of cancer. He had a healthy philosophy: "You pray with all the faith you have, and then you leave the results to God." The church stayed in a place of childlike faith, resting in the goodness of God and continuing to walk in faith for the next person who needed prayer. God healed many people over the next few years, including two of our children. I have seen other churches face similar situations where everyone had faithfully joined together in prayer and had seen loved ones die. Instead of resting in the goodness of God, there began a journey of questions. "What did we do wrong?" "Should we even believe in healing?" "Why did this happen?" They even evaluated their theology, what they believe about God, from their place of pain. The leaders went into what I would call a crisis of faith and dragged many of their congregants with them.

When our heart doesn't understand what is happening and God's mysteries seem too complex, we can be like the Psalmist:

Lord, my heart is meek before you.
I don't consider myself better than others.
I'm content to not pursue matters that are over my head—
such as your complex mysteries and wonders—
that I'm not yet ready to understand.
I am humbled and quieted in your presence.
Like a contented child who rests on its mother's lap,
I'm your resting child and my soul is content in you
(Psalm 131:1–2 TPT).

God is mysterious, and we will not always understand His ways. To pray for people's healing is risky business! If you pray for someone to be blessed, there is no absolute way to measure if God answers that prayer. We can live in a place of not looking for results, knowing that eventually, in heaven, all our prayers will be answered. This is not the case when praying for people to be healed. Either they are, or they aren't. God likes us to step out into the place of utter dependence on Him. In my own ability, I might give someone some good advice or counsel. I might be able, in my own kindness, to encourage someone who is discouraged. I can give money to someone who has a material need, but in my own flesh, I cannot heal anyone. God *must* be involved. In fact, I need to learn to be a funnel through which His power flows.

> *I need to learn to be a funnel through which His power flows.*

Agnes Sanford, in her book *The Healing Light*, gives some great principles for releasing healing. God used her to release an extraordinary number of healings beginning in the 1940s and 1950s.

The first step then in seeking help from God is to contact God. "Be still and know that I am God."

Let us then lay aside our worries and cares, quiet our minds and concentrate upon the reality of God. So, the first step is to relax and to remind ourselves that there is a source of life outside of ourselves.

The second step is to turn it on, by some such prayer as this, "Heavenly Father, please increase in me at this time Your life-giving power." Or if we do not know this outside life as our Heavenly Father, we can simply say "Whoever you are—whatever you are—come into me now!" *(She did this as she helped those, who were not sure if they believed in God, receive healing.)*

The third step is to believe that this power is coming into us and to accept it by faith. No matter how much we ask for something it becomes ours only as we accept it and give thanks for it. "Thank You," we can say, "that this life is now coming into me and increasing life in my spirit and in my mind and in my body."

And the fourth step is to observe the operations of that light and life. In order to do so, we must decide on some tangible thing that we wish accomplished by that power so that we can know without question whether our experiment succeeded or failed.[4]

Agnes Sanford thought praying for healing was the simplest type of prayer. Seeing clearly whether the prayer was answered helped her to build her faith. Faith grows when we can see our prayers answered. She was doing this in a part of the body of Christ that normally saw very few healings.

We might be praying from a place of faith but may have forgotten a key component. Paul points out in Galatians 5:6 (MSG), "For in Christ, neither our most conscientious religion nor disregard of religion amounts to anything. What matters is something far more interior: faith expressed in love." Or as it says in The Amplified Version, "but only faith activated *and* energized *and* expressed *and* working through love." Jesus exemplifies this is Mark 1:41 (NLT) and Matthew 20:34 (NASB), where he is moved with compassion as he reaches out to heal. Agnes Sanford says it this way:

> Then if we would help man through intercession, we must hold God by one hand and man by the other hand, never separating ourselves either from the love of God or from the love of man. As we do this by the indwelling of Jesus Christ, God can work through our normal human love in ways that we do not see . . . Because we love His little ones in a simple human way, a way that they can understand, because we so love them in all their weakness and stupidity and suffering, they love us. And because they love us, they feel the healing love of the Father shining through the human love of little hearts. Thus our simple human love will be used for divine purposes.[5]

This could apply to every area of our prayer life, not just healing. The key is love.

Father God,

I want to be a funnel for Your love and healing power. Forgive me for any way I have limited You or made You small in my eyes. Forgive me for thinking You don't desire to heal miraculously anymore. Forgive me where I have focused on "believing right" and have forgotten to love. Baptize me again with Your love, that I would love others the way You do. In Jesus' Name, Amen.

Symptom	Potential Problem	Try this Solution
My prayers are not answered.	People are not being healed.	Believe He can use you.
	Do not know how to flow in healing.	Become a funnel of His presence, power, glory, and love.

Troubleshooting Guide
For
My Prayers
Are Not Answered

Symptom	Potential Problem	Try this Solution	Chapter
My prayers are not answered.	Believing or living contrary to Scripture.	Change your mindsets or behavior.	13
My prayers are not answered.	No faith in the atmosphere.	Change the atmosphere. Release testimonies.	14
My prayers are not answered.	Negativity	Cut the negative waves. Be accountable. Ask tough questions to expose the root.	15
My prayers are not answered.	Praying prayers to try to control another person's choices or circumstances.	Let go of control. Submit to God	16

My prayers are not answered.	Mundane prayers.	Seek freshness. Do something different. Keep track of your prayers and the answers.	17
My prayers are not answered.	Giving up too soon. Forgetting to be persistent.	Be alert. Finish the assignment.	18
My prayers are not answered.	Lonely prayers. Prayers lacking agreement.	Find a prayer partner or group.	19
My prayers are not answered.	Prayer without action.	You may be part of the answer to what you are praying. Is God waiting for you to do something?	20
My prayers are not answered.	Seeking the blessings of God without seeking God the Father.	Spend time focusing on the face of God instead of what you desire for Him to give you.	21
My prayers are not answered.	Doubting God's ability to use someone like me.	Realize God uses ordinary clay jars.	22
My prayers are not answered.	People are not being healed. Do not know how to flow in healing.	Believe He can use you. Become a funnel of His presence, power, glory, and love.	23

Regular Maintenance

For Your
Prayer Life

Chapter 24
Peace: The New Normal

Our church friends, I'll call them Don and Stephanie, had a beautiful family. Don worked hard at a blue-collar job to successfully support his family. Everyone was so excited about Stephanie's sleek, new-to-her car. It was a beautiful Cadillac and she loved it. Less than a year later, I came into a Wednesday night church dinner and several people were whispering at the table as I sat down. They smiled at me and quickly took me into their confidence. Stephanie let her car run out of oil, and it burned up the motor. She didn't know it needed regular maintenance. Poor Stephanie was embarrassed by what she did not know.

Cars aren't the only thing that needs regular maintenance. How many of us have burned up our spiritual motors by ignoring basic maintenance? We want to do the basic maintenance so we can diagnose when we are abiding in negative emotions and worry instead of the peace of Christ.

My Grandma Leap was a worrier. She "pray-worried" her prayers: half prayer, half worry. This is normal for many believers. It's not what Jesus desires, but it is prevalent. "Anxiety has become the number one mental health issue in North America. It's estimated that one third of the North American adult population experiences problems with anxiety."[1] For many in our culture, inside and outside the church, anxious is the new normal." Many are continually in a place of anxiety, which leads to peace being rare or non-existent in their lives.

Jesus is the Prince of Peace. If He lives in us and we abide in Him, peace ought to be normal for us, but many of us are living a divided life, one in which we know what is right, and yet we are living a different way. We desire to live in holiness and purity but find ourselves doing the very thing we hate to do (see Romans 7:18–19). It is hard to be at peace while living any kind of divided life. Those who have given their lives to Jesus will find it difficult to be at peace while running from God. Being at peace is crucial to living this walk with Jesus. He uses peace and the lack of peace to communicate with us.

We want to be so grounded in the peace of God that when we are not at peace, we know we need to ask the Lord why we are in a place of worry or unrest.

We want to be so grounded in the peace of God that when we are not at peace, we know we need to ask the Lord why we are in a place of worry or unrest. As Paul states in Colossians, "And let the peace that comes from Christ rule in your hearts. For as members of one body you are called to live in peace" (Colossians 3:15 NLT). With peace, we can live above our actual circumstances. Peace becomes our new normal.

Meditating on Scripture and memorizing verses can help us change our mindsets from worry to peace. One of the Holy Spirit's jobs is to bring things to remembrance (see John 14:26). The more we know the word of God, the more He can help us get realigned to His will. As we ponder verses about peace, we give the Holy Spirit permission to remind us of these verses when we become anxious.

And everything I've taught you is so that the peace which is in me will be in you and will give you great confidence as you rest in me. For in this unbelieving world you will experience trouble and sorrows, but you must be courageous, for I have conquered the world! (John 16:33 TPT)

For the mind-set of the flesh is death, but the mind-set controlled by the Spirit finds life and peace. (Romans 8:6 TPT)

I leave the gift of peace with you—my peace. Not the kind of fragile peace given by the world, but my perfect peace. Don't yield to fear or be troubled in your hearts—instead, be courageous! (John 14:27 TPT)

There is such a great peace and well-being that comes to the lovers of your word, and they will never be offended. (Psalm 119:165 TPT)

You will keep in perfect peace all who trust in you, all whose thoughts are fixed on you! (Isaiah 26:3 NLT)

During the Coronavirus pandemic, Natalie Grant and her daughter Gracie released a song on Facebook that Gracie wrote when she was nine years old. Within three days it had almost two million views. The song struck a chord with an anxious, unsure population that was locked away because of a virus that couldn't be seen or understood. The theme of the song is to turn the things we are concerned about into prayers. We have so many thoughts going through our minds that it is a challenge to know which are true, which are exaggerated, and even which ones are lies. As these concerns appear, we don't dwell on them, but transition to prayer. I think this is the meaning of 1 Thessalonians 5:17 (MSG), "pray all the time," or in *The Passion Translation*, "Make your life a prayer." Yes, we pray in our prayer closet, but we also want to keep a running dialogue with the Lord.

It is good to recognize where we are emotionally. When we aren't at peace, we need to acknowledge what we are feeling. We might be worried or fearful or stressed. Next, we look up, fix our eyes on Him, and realize this is a spiritual battle, and He is one who specializes in divine exchanges. Please don't make it complicated, our prayers can be simple.

When we accept where we are emotionally, we can then ask God for a divine exchange. This may look like:

- Turn Worry into Trust: Lord, I feel so worried about this situation. Forgive me for worrying. You are trustworthy and I choose to put my trust back in You. I lay this situation at Your feet.

- Turn Fear into Peace: Lord, I am feeling fearful. I can't walk in fear and faith at the same time. Lord, Your Word says perfect love casts out fear (see 1 John 4:18 NKJV), so I am asking Your perfect love to cast out this fear. I choose to set my eyes on You, come out of agreement with this fear, and walk in peace and faith.

- Turn Striving into Rest: Lord, I sense I am striving to accomplish what is in front of me. Your Word says I am to strive to enter Your rest (see Hebrews 4:11 ESV), so I shift from striving for acceptance and victory to striving to enter Your rest. I choose to make every effort to operate from the place of peace.

You may be feeling a negative emotion, but you are unsure what to ask the Lord to replace it with. If you look up the negative emotion in a dictionary app and then look for the antonyms, it is amazing how revelatory this can be. You can then look up the positive emotion in the Word of God. Focus on the Lord and what His word says about this emotion until your emotions shift. We want to not only get rid of the negative emotion, we want to also replenish our hearts with its opposite.

Corrie Ten Boom reminds us of the futility of worry. "Worrying is carrying tomorrow's load with today's strength—carrying two days at once. It is moving into tomorrow ahead of time. Worrying doesn't empty tomorrow of its sorrow, it empties today of its strength."[2]

Father God,

I want to turn my cares into prayers. Thank You for being willing to carry my burdens. In the midst of all the turmoil and fear in our world today, would You please teach me to get above the fray and abide in You in that place of peace? Help me to be aware of the stress I am carrying. I declare stress and worry are not my portion. Lead me to the place of peace. Create a new normal for me full of peace and calm. In Jesus' Name, Amen.

Chapter 25
Who's on the Throne?

Picture with me a throne positioned in your heart. Whoever sits on the throne is in charge and calls the shots. Could be you, could be Jesus, could be anyone. Although there is not a physical throne in our hearts, we do enthrone the Lord when we submit to His Lordship. Jesus is on the throne of our life. *We enthrone the Lord when we submit to His Lordship.* Our self is yielding to Christ, and our interests are directed by Him, resulting in harmony with God's plan.

Some profess to be Christians who don't necessarily have Jesus on the throne of their hearts. It is a choice, a daily, moment by moment choice. There are times when, because of a lack of attentiveness, or because of trauma or our desire to perform, we crawl back up on the throne of our lives ourselves. Depending on ourselves and what we know or succumbing to a religious spirit to guide us not only affects the way we live but also the way we pray.

Jesus promised us a Helper (John 14:16), or as some versions say, a Counselor, who will abide with us. Depending on the Helper to help us or the Counselor to counsel us has an amazingly positive impact on our prayer life.

Let's discuss how people can get to that place of self-effort and being on the throne of their own lives and how it affects their prayer life.

Different Throne Positions and How it Affects our Prayers

The Person who has received Christ as their Savior but does not understand the importance of cooperating with the Holy Spirit.	How This Person Prays
A key component of prayer is co-laboring with the Holy Spirit to know what to pray and how to pray.

Many people who come to Jesus don't understand the gift of the Holy Spirit and end up walking out their Christian life, including their prayer life, from a place of self-effort. These people do this from a place of ignorance; they just don't know. | This person will pray from the depth of their knowledge of Scripture and the longings of their heart. If they know the Word, they can pray in agreement with the Word, but without leaning on the Holy Spirit, they may miss the strategies of the Lord. These prayers often will be answered, but Jesus gave the Holy Spirit the name Helper. How much more effective our prayers can be with the help of the Helper! Ask the Holy Spirit to fill you and guide you. Pause and listen for His direction as you pray. |

The Believer with a Religious Spirit	How the Believer with a Religious Spirit Prays
Some have come to Jesus and have been taught to avoid much of the workings of the Holy Spirit. Yes, the Holy Spirit is part of the Trinity, but kind of like the black sheep of the family, He shouldn't be given too much attention or deference. There are people all across the body of Christ who have come under the influence of a religious spirit. A religious spirit is a demonic spirit that tries to imitate the work of the Holy Spirit. It seeks to influence people or groups to replace a genuine relationship with God with good works and habitual religious customs. These spirits can and do affect them and how they pray.	Praying "right" becomes the focus of those controlled by a religious spirit. Their focus can be on correct form and wording more than seeing God move. They may feel guilty if they miss their prayer time and may even fear something horrible will happen to their children because they missed praying for them for one day. These spirits are controlling and make life heavy and burdensome, and they can make prayer meetings the same. What if we don't pray for everything or everyone? Often prayer times, whether individual or corporate, led by those controlled by this spirit are so wearying and boring that prayer becomes a low priority and shame burdens those who quit praying.

We must come out of agreement with this spirit. For example, we can pray, "I repent for each and every time I have knowingly or unknowingly partnered with the spirit of religion. In the name of Jesus, I renounce and break every agreement with the spirit of religion. I speak to the spirit of religion and tell it to go in Jesus' name." After this prayer, ask for the Holy Spirit to fill you, and ask Him to guide your prayers.

The Carnal Believer	How the Carnal Person Prays
Others come to Jesus, embrace the fulness of the Holy Spirit, and submit to the leadership of the Holy Spirit. Jesus is on the throne of their lives, but then, every so often, their flesh rears up and they jump back onto the throne of their lives. This happens to all of us. We repent, and the Lord is once again in charge. If we are not careful, we yield more and more to our flesh over time, get lax in our repentance, and before long, the abnormal becomes normal and we are no longer living a submitted life. We are living and praying from a carnal, fleshly place. Our will becomes more important than God's will. This has become our new normal.	The prayer life of this type of person can go several directions. If the flesh reigns and worldly sin is involved, many times the person just quits praying. They don't want to think about God. They hope that if they don't draw attention to themselves, God won't know what they are up to. If the flesh involved is more acceptable in Christian circles, like pride, gossip, worry, or fear, they may pray more, but usually from a place of, "God, let me tell you what You need to do to fix this situation, so that I can be more comfortable or prosperous, or things can be peaceful around me." If a person is eloquent and "a good pray-er" they may actually pray more, especially in public settings, because they enjoy the limelight their prayers draw. We are always just one prayer of repentance away from the Lord returning to the throne of our lives and His lordship being re-established in our lives.

The Traumatized Believer

Still others come to Jesus, embrace the fullness of the Spirit, and learn to live a submitted lifestyle. A traumatic event occurs like a death, serious illness, a spouse cheating, or a child falling away from the Lord. During the pain, confusion, and feeling out of control, they climb up on the throne of their life and grasp for anything they can control. They didn't intend to dethrone the Lord from their lives, but in their devastating place, instead of yielding to the Lord, they grabbed onto the control handles of their lives.

How the Traumatized Believer Prays

This dear brother or sister may still pray out of desperation, but many times disappointment or hope deferred will cloud their prayers. They may still pray in faith for others, for leaders or nations, but not for their own family and situations. They can become divided in their hearts or faith. They may still believe God is good in a general sort of way and know He loves the world, but feelings of unworthiness or disappointment cause them to doubt God's goodness in their own lives. They think there is something that keeps Him from intervening on their behalf. God is willing to answer their prayers, but they might need some healing and deliverance from the spirit of trauma or disappointment.

The Believer who Performs	How the Performer Prays
This person starts off well. They know the Lord intimately and live a yielded lifestyle. The Lord starts to use them, and they become recognized as someone who walks with the Lord and hears His voice. People want to hear what they have to say. People want to meet with them. They become well known in their circle of influence. It does not matter how big that circle is. It could be a whole nation or a small church. The key is that within their circle, they are big. Before long, they get busy doing things for the Lord. They begin to believe what others are saying about them, and their time with Jesus gets hurried and shallow. They never intended to let their ministry take the place of Jesus on the throne of their lives. It just happened. Pride may have helped, or maybe Satan's flattery worked. It could just be busyness. The gifting, calling, and anointing are still there. But they start to operate out of the gifting instead of out of their intimacy with Jesus.	This person might see many prayers answered because they have learned to cooperate with the gifts of the Spirit, but they are in a dangerous place. Jesus desires intimacy with us, not performance from us. Perhaps a season of pressing into the Lord, alone and in private, would be helpful. A suitable place to start for these people is to pray from a place of humility: "Forgive me Lord, let me fall in love with You all over again. It is You I want to please."

Peace comes from knowing we are rightly positioned with the Lord and listening to His guidance through the Holy Spirit. Again, this does not guarantee our every prayer will be answered immediately, but we at least know we have done our part.

Father God,

Lord, we choose for you to be on the throne of our hearts. We know that the only place for us on that throne is in Your lap. We surrender and let You rule and reign in our hearts. Lord, help us to not see others in these lists, but help us to see any way that we might be in any of these lists. We desire to pray and live out of a place of peace, intimacy, revelation with You. We want to partner with You to be an effective prayer warrior for You. In Jesus' Name, Amen

Chapter 26
Fully Loved and Accepted

O ur insecurities, weaknesses, and failures are ever before us, and we can see them so easily. They can crowd out the reality of how Jesus sees us and can limit our prayer life. My friend Joseph Winger, who has been a prayer warrior for decades, recently found that during the first part of his prayer time, he was wading through accusations and general thoughts of malaise as he approached the throne. It is difficult to approach Father God with confidence if the accuser is filling our mind with all the ways we don't measure up. We don't have the boldness, confidence, and faith needed to make requests of the Lord. This didn't just happen overnight, but Joseph noticed that more and more of his prayer time was being used to deal with these accusations. Joseph shifted his prayer time by starting it with the declaration, "I am the righteousness of God in Christ Jesus" (based on 2 Corinthians 5:21). This decree silenced the accuser and cleared the atmosphere of the slime and accusations. His prayer time shifted from wasting time dealing with the condemnation of the enemy to boldly communicating with the Lord from a place of confidence and faith. Not confidence in himself or his works, but confidence in his position in Christ. "My delightfully loved friends, when our hearts don't condemn us, we have a bold freedom to speak face-to-face with God" (1 John 3:21 TPT).

"For God made the only one who did not know sin to become sin for us, so that we might become the righteousness of God through our union with him" (2 Corinthians 5:21 TPT). We read that verse, but do we fully grasp it? Try reading it again. Here is my paraphrase: "For God made Jesus sin for us, so we who weren't righteous could actually become the righteousness of God, because we are in union with Jesus." Not only am I the righteousness of God in Christ Jesus, I also am fully loved and accepted.

> And so we know and rely on the love God has for us (1 John 4:16).

> And we know (understand, recognize, are conscious of, by observation and by experience) and believe (adhere to and put faith in and rely on) the love God cherishes for us (1 John 4:16 AMPC).

The Greek word for "know" in 1 John 4:16 is *ginosko*. It is a word rich with meanings, but one of them is "to come to know by experience."[1] Thayer's Lexicon lists one of its definitions as, "To recognize as worthy of intimacy and love."[2] This is not just book knowledge where I read in the Bible, "God loves me." This is stated more fully, "As I live this walk with the Lord, I realize how much God loves me. He pursues me. He desires me to feel His love for me" (my translation). We don't just know it, but as The Amplified Version states, "we understand, recognize, and are conscious of, by observation and by experience," the love and acceptance of God the Father.

Many of us relate to Jesus, our friend and brother, more than we relate to God the Father. Perhaps we had positive experiences with our friends and brothers, but maybe our father was distant, absent, harsh, or abusive. We may not have experienced the love of an earthly father, so it is natural to project those feelings onto our

Heavenly Father. Ask Him to show you how much He loves you. He loves to answer this prayer!

Knowing how much God loves us is one of the keys to praying with boldness. If I see myself as an orphan, I will come from the mindset of an orphan, but if I see myself as a co-heir with Christ, it totally changes my perspective.

The mature children of God are those who are moved by the impulses of the Holy Spirit. And you did not receive the "spirit of religious duty," leading you back into the fear of *never being good enough.* But you have received the "Spirit of full acceptance," enfolding you into the family of God. And you will never feel orphaned, for as he rises up within us, our spirits join him in saying the words of tender affection, "Beloved Father!" For the Holy Spirit makes God's fatherhood real to us as he whispers into our innermost being, "You are God's beloved child!"

And since we are his true children, we qualify to share all his treasures, for indeed, we are heirs of God himself. And since we are joined to Christ, we also inherit all that he is and all that he has. We will experience being co-glorified with him provided that we accept his sufferings as our own (Romans 8:14–17 TPT).

How encouraging for us that Jesus made provision for us to move from a spirit of fear or slavery into a spirit of adoption or full acceptance. What a glorious exchange is available to all of us who will receive it. This shift will totally change our mindset, but it is not just a transition in our brain; it is a spiritual exchange. We move from serving and working for Jesus to gain acceptance and love to serving and working because we are loved and accepted. An orphan lives from the mindset of measuring themselves or others, believing there is not enough love or mon-

We move from working for Jesus to gain acceptance and love to working because we are loved and accepted.

ey or ministry opportunities for everyone, so we need to battle for what we need.

A person measuring may think like this:

- Am I good enough?
- Am I better than that person?
- She is so much better at _____than I am.
- Do I sing, dance, write, or pray better than her?
- She probably wouldn't like me; she is so much more _____ than me.
- Am I loved?

On the other hand, the sons and daughters who understand their full acceptance as a child of God know they are co-heirs with Christ. They understand their worth is not dependent on their performance. They are able to accept others' victories without feeling less and others' difficulties without feeling somehow superior.

As Henri Nouwen states in *The Life of the Beloved,* "The real 'work' of prayer is to become silent and listen to the voice that says good things about me."[3]

"For it was always in his perfect plan to adopt us as his delightful children, through our union with Jesus, the Anointed One, so that his tremendous love that cascades over us would glorify his grace—*for the same love he has for his Beloved One, Jesus, he has for us.* And this unfolding plan brings him great pleasure!" (Ephesians 1:5–6 TPT, emphasis added).

If this concept of orphan to sonship is new to you, I would recommend *Spiritual Slavery to Spiritual Sonship: Your Destiny Awaits You* by Jack Frost.[4]

Father God,

Establish me in the place of fully understanding that I am a co-heir to Christ, fully accepted and fully loved, just as I am. I have to admit it is hard for my mind to understand how You love me with the same love You have for Jesus, but I choose to receive it in my spirit. I declare, "You love me, Father God, with the same love You have for Jesus." Your word says "...that love which You have bestowed on Me may be in them (felt in their hearts) and I (Myself) may be in them" (John 17:26 AMPC). Help me to not feel loved when things are going well but then falter from that place when things are tough. Especially help me when I am not seeing immediate responses to my heart-felt prayers. I want to walk in a deep trust, knowing that You have my best in mind. I want to focus my attention on Your love and kindness. I acknowledge You have a better perspective than I do. In Jesus' Name, Amen.

Chapter 27

Watch Over Your Heart

We had tried and tried to get a new position in a different church. My husband, Jack, had sent resumes everywhere he could think of without a single response. I could understand if there had just been a few responses and Jack's credentials or gift mix weren't right for the job. But nothing. God was trying to do a deep work in us, and if we had jumped out of our current situation, we might have had to go around the mountain again until we learned the lesson. Easy to see on this side of history, but at the time, it was not clear. We felt hurt, offended, and taken advantage of. During this time, God was still miraculously providing for us.

We could relate to the disciples in Mark 6. They had just seen Jesus take five loaves and two fish, feed five thousand men and their families, and still have twelve baskets of leftovers. Talk about miraculous provision! After leaving them, He went up on a mountainside to pray.

> Later that night, the boat was in the middle of the lake, and he was alone on land. He saw the disciples straining at the oars, *because the wind was against them.* Shortly before dawn

he went out to them, walking on the lake. He was about to pass by them, but when they saw him walking on the lake, they thought he was a ghost. They cried out, because they all saw him and were terrified.

Immediately he spoke to them and said, "Take courage! It is I. Don't be afraid." Then he climbed into the boat with them, and the wind died down. They were completely amazed, for they had not understood about the loaves; their hearts were hardened (Mark 6:47-52, emphasis added).

While rowing against the wind, in times of difficulty, it is easy for our hearts to become hardened. In *The Amplified Version,* verse 52 states, "For they failed to consider *or* understand [the teaching and meaning of the miracle of] the loaves; [in fact] their hearts had grown callous [had become dull and had lost the power of understanding]."

Brian Simmons, the translator of *The Passion Translation*, points out in the footnotes that there were two lessons the Lord was trying to teach the disciples with the loaves and the fishes. One was "that Jesus had all power to meet every need," and the other was "that the disciples carried this power with them, for the bread multiplied in their hands."[1] He also pointed out that when the disciples were described with a hard heart, they were said to be "unwilling to accept new information."[2] Wow! Take a moment and consider this: Are we willing to take in new information? Are we so set in our theology that even if God himself is trying to whisper something in our ears we resist it? Sometimes we have a little box in our brain or heart where we keep all we know or believe about God, and if we are presented with anything new it must fit in those little boxes. When we are rowing against the wind, it is difficult to hear the Lord whisper His perspective. All we hear is the sound of the waves, our recitation of all the hard things we are facing, and maybe even our own faithless prayers. Pause and think about it.

There have been times I prayed for understanding and insight but wasn't willing (or even aware of my need) to deal with my hardened and calloused heart. If I want to keep God in the little box that I have fashioned for Him, I could be operating with a hardened heart. Maybe we need to repent for thinking we know how God wants to work in a situation. Do I think that God only works in ways that line up with my or my church's traditions? Often, this is how a religious spirit works. We must come out of agreement with this spirit. For example, we can pray, "I repent for each and every time I have knowingly or unknowingly partnered with the spirit of religion. In the name of Jesus, I renounce and break every agreement with the spirit of religion. I speak to the spirit of religion and tell it to go in Jesus' name."

We need to deal with what is seen on the surface, but also be aware of what lurks underneath. Look for the root issues and inquire of the Lord about what is going on deep down. It is easy, yet unprofitable, to skim the surface in our prayers. Go deep! The Lord will help us.

In the last half of Ezekiel 36, God speaks through the prophet Ezekiel about how Israel has defiled the land and gone after other gods, but His desire is to renew and restore them for His own name's sake. He begins this process by sprinkling them clean and then giving them a new heart.

> I'll pour pure water over you and scrub you clean. I'll give you a new heart, put a new spirit in you. I'll remove the stone heart from your body and replace it with a heart that's God-willed, not self-willed. I'll put my Spirit in you and make it possible for you to do what I tell you and live by my commands. You'll once again live in the land I gave your ancestors. You'll be my people! I'll be your God! (Ezekiel 36:25-28 MSG).

We too can begin the process of renewal and restoration by receiving a new heart, what The New Living Translation calls a "tender, responsive heart."

The Lord will help us, but we also need to do our part. "Above all else, guard your heart, for everything you do flows from it" (Proverbs 4:23). "Above all else, watch over your heart; diligently guard it because from a sincere and pure heart come the good and noble things of life" (Proverbs 4:23 Voice). When I first came to Jesus, I was taught that Proverbs 4:23 was a dating verse. Teachers encouraged us to watch over our hearts, to not give our hearts too freely to others, to keep us from being hurt. What a great application of the verse, but there is so much more to it. We need to watch over our hearts our whole life and in every situation.

Before going deeper into watching over our heart, I would like to go on a little side trip that will help to understand the ways of God in a broader sense. Stephen Crosby states in *Authority, Accountability and the Apostolic Movement:*

> Perceptual tension is divinely designed into God's Word. The entire book consists of principles and emphases in complementary or competing tension. Like two sides of a coin, many themes in the Word seem at first glance to be polar opposites.
>
> Apparent contradictions disappear when we understand the principle of antinomy. Antinomy describes two statements, conclusions, laws, or principles that seem equally logical, reasonable, or necessary but exist in irresolvable conflict or contradiction with each other.
>
> Most heretical teaching and improper emphasis results from attempting to undo or resolve divinely designed antinomies. God's word is like an elastic band; it only functions in tension. When considered in tension and totality, God's word coheres. Release the tension through intellectual jockeying

and no end of doctrinal strangeness will result. This is not a left or right wing, conservative or liberal, traditionalist or modernist issue. Aberrations, imbalance, over and under emphasis occur across the Christian landscape.[3]

The Word of God is not a rule book; it is the living Word. We need the Holy Spirit with us when we are reading and studying His Word. Maybe you have heard the joke about the guy who is seeking the Lord for guidance, and he closes his eyes, flips open his Bible and points to a verse, and it says, "Judas hung himself." The guy was distraught and said, "Lord, I need another verse." He opened the Bible again to "Go and do likewise." Satan himself quotes scripture in the temptation of Jesus in Matthew 4. Satan loves to use Scripture applied at the wrong place or the wrong time. Christians can be influenced by a religious spirit when we naively handle the Word of God without the essential leading of the Holy Spirit.

Christians can be influenced by a religious spirit when we naively handle the Word of God without the essential leading of the Holy Spirit.

Now, let's look at some examples of this tension between living in the spirit and the flesh:

- Jesus is fully God and fully man.
- Overlook an offense, but also openly rebuke.
- In the world, but not of the world.
- Seated in the heavens, but on earth.
- Dead, but alive.
- Slaves, but free.
- Poor, but rich.

When we camp at one end of these tensions, we are susceptible to having our vision distorted. We can get tunnel vision or short-sightedness. How and what we see affects how we pray.

Let's look at the tension between dying to self and watching over our heart with all diligence, which I might define as living with a heart that is wholehearted and free. I remember watching a YouTube video years ago, and an unnamed intercessor shared that she saw that Jesus was desiring to clean our hearts. To do so, He needed to turn it inside out so that He could clean all the crevices. The problem was that turning it inside out would cause us to die. Paul speaks of this in his letter to the Galatians.

> What actually took place is this: I tried keeping rules and working my head off to please God, and it didn't work. So I quit being a "law man" so that I could be *God's* man. Christ's life showed me how, and enabled me to do it. I identified myself completely with him. Indeed, I have been crucified with Christ. My ego is no longer central. It is no longer important that I appear righteous before you or have your good opinion, and I am no longer driven to impress God. Christ lives in me. The life you see me living is not "mine," but it is lived by faith in the Son of God, who loved me and gave himself for me. I am not going to go back on that (Galatians 2:19-21a MSG).

Dying to self is crucial to living this life with Jesus. To truly clean our hearts, we must die. We can't pick up offenses, hang onto our rights, or worry about our reputation. Dead people don't have rights or even reputations that they can preserve. We can't watch over our hearts from a place of self- preservation or self-promotion.

I knew a woman who didn't feel as if she had a voice in her early life, nor in her marriage. She divorced her husband and rebuilt her life but from a place of self-preservation. In many ways she was successful, but she still lived from an inner conflict. One cannot successfully walk with Christ and walk in a place of self-preservation.

One of my mentors gave me advice when she felt I was overly concerned about making mistakes: "You can only die once. Just get it over, have the funeral, and move on." I agree you can only die once, but wow, can our flesh fight for life!

Do you see the tension? We are called to die, but we are to watch over our hearts, for from them flow the issues of life. We are called to die, but we want our hearts to be alive and emotionally whole.

If we follow Jesus' example of dying, we see He did it courageously, with forgiveness, without excuses, without defending his own reputation, with concern for others, with eternity in mind, willingly, and with his flesh being ripped off. Wow, what an example.

Let me make this clear: A single grain of wheat will never be more than a single grain of wheat unless it drops into the ground and dies. Because then it sprouts and produces a great harvest of wheat—all because one grain died. The person who loves his life and pampers himself will miss true life! But the one who detaches his life from this world and abandons himself to me, will find true life and enjoy it forever (John 12:24-25 TPT)!

To die, and yet live. To live in a whole-hearted place watching over our heart. Bestselling author Brené Brown states in *Daring Greatly*:

Wholehearted living is about engaging in our lives from a place of worthiness. It means cultivating the courage, compassion, and connection to wake up in the morning and think, *no matter what gets done and how much gets left undone, I am enough*. It's going to bed at night thinking, *Yes, I am imperfect and vulnerable and sometimes afraid, but that doesn't change the truth that I am also brave and worthy of love and belonging*.[4]

Part of our daily maintenance is watching over our hearts. Are my feelings engaged? Do I feel joy, sadness, anger, grief, and happiness? Or have I shut down my emotions? Prayer is not just spirit to spirit; our emotions are involved. The Lord will guide us by using our emotions. We submit our emotions to the Holy Spirit and work to keep our emotions healed.

- Do I need to forgive someone? After extending forgiveness, have I dealt with the pain, or did I just stuff it?
- How is my self-talk? Is it critical and full of what I should do or can't do?
- Am I overly concerned with what others are thinking of me?

As we follow Jesus' example of dying, and learn from others such as Brené Brown about living from a wholehearted place, we find a balance between dying to self and watching over our heart. This is not something we learn about and instantaneously implement, then quickly check it off our to-do list. Instead, it is a destination we journey toward as we walk with Jesus.

If we are struggling through a difficult time with someone we love, and we desire to pray for them, every time we pray, we touch the pain. The deeper the pain and the longer the wait for the answer to our prayers, the more tempted we are to avoid the pain by avoiding prayer. The problem then changes. We then start to deal with the difficult situation without the Lord's help. Not a good plan, but sometimes the pain is so intense we just try to avoid feeling it instead of pressing through it.

I was excited to be having tea with my good friend Anne Evans. She and her late husband Tim have written several wonderful books on marriage. We were enjoying our "girl time" when Anne slipped on her counselor hat. She reached across the table for a pad of paper and then she drew the shape of a heart. Next, she divided it into about ten sections, and in those sections, she wrote out some of my significant life experiences. Some good and some bad.

She explained, "If one pocket is left to fester, it becomes a pain pocket. Bad experiences can be healed through counseling, deliverance, and applying the Word of God, so these pockets are not leaking out and affecting us." She added, "These pain pockets can define our relationships, including how we interact with God in our prayer life. We must be careful not to define ourselves or let others define us by these pain pockets."

I kind of dismissed one of the pockets where she had written one of my life experiences. I was downplaying it and added a comment. "Well, that is just the way it is." She glanced up at me and replied, "Yes, but that doesn't mean you didn't deserve to have what you didn't receive."

I was challenged because I had forgiven, but I hadn't dealt with the pain or residue that was still there that needed to receive healing. I had just let it fester. Maybe a slower fester than if I hadn't forgiven what had happened, but I hadn't taken my heart to the Lord for healing. He let me see an area of my heart that needed healing and unlocking.

Our defeats and victories do not define us! Jesus defines us from the place of His incredible love. In Song of Solomon 5:4, the Shulamite woman pulled back from her bridegroom; some versions call her the sleeping bride. She may have pulled back in fear or pain, but her beloved pursued her just like Jesus pursues us. She describes it as, "My beloved reached into me to unlock my heart. The core of my very being trembled at His touch" (Song of Songs 5:4 TPT). Even in those places where we are shut down for whatever reason, He pursues us and unlocks our heart.

Please don't just quickly read the above questions and this prayer, instead, take time with Jesus to ponder these questions. Let my prayer be a stepping stone to your own heartfelt prayer.

Dear Lord,

You know the deep things of my heart, the things I can't see or acknowledge. I trust You to search my heart and reveal everything that is hindering our relationship and my ability to partner with You in prayer. Bring it to the light. Go for the root issues, Lord. Help me see when I am wearing my temporary glasses, instead of seeing things from an eternal perspective. I don't want to be like the 3-year-old that just wants what I want without any thought of what is truly for my good. Heal the broken and hardened places in my heart. Reveal selfishness and shortsightedness. Show me where I have settled for a repentance that comes from embarrassment more than sorrow that I have offended You, a Holy and just God. Father God, would you do Ezekiel 36:26 (Voice) in my life? "I will plant a new heart and new spirit inside of you. I will take out your stubborn, stony heart and give you a willing, tender heart of flesh." In Jesus' Name, Amen.

Remember the goal of all this maintenance is to live from a place of peace. Peace should be our norm. If we normally are at peace, it will be easier to notice when we become unsettled or anxious or worried. Furthermore, we will know it is time to do some maintenance.

Chapter 28

Types of Prayer

When Jack and I were young and newly married often we didn't have the money to pay a mechanic to work on our cars. Long before there were YouTube videos to teach people how to fix cars, we found a book with directions on how to work on our specific car. Jack would read the book, figure out what to do, and head out to work on the car. Before long, he would come back in the house, frustrated because he rarely had the correct tool.

About fifteen years later, we moved into a neighborhood where our neighbor was an amazing mechanic with a full array of tools, which he was generously willing to share. Our neighbor had been seriously injured from an accident and could no longer work on cars. From his lawn chair, he sat and helped Jack fix our vehicles. He knew what needed to be done and would tell Jack which tool to use for each situation. Working on the car moved from being a frustrating, draining experience to a much more peaceful and effective experience.

The Holy Spirit works much like our mechanic friend. He knows what needs to be done to "fix" a situation and He knows which tools we need to use. It is our responsibility to know what "tools of prayer" are available and how to use them. If you ask a mechanic what the most important tool is, the answer would be "the one you need right now." Just like there are many types of tools, there are also different types of prayer.

When I was first exposed to prayer, I thought the only type of prayer was me asking God to do something or give me something. Although this is one type of prayer, it is not the only type of prayer. If that is the only type of prayer I know, it is like trying to fix a car using only a hammer. A hammer is very effective in the right setting, but not really helpful when working on a car. Knowing which types of prayer are available and how to pray in these different ways gives us a strong and peaceful foundation in our prayer lives.

The key to prayer of any kind, in any setting, at any level, is that the prayer is led by the Holy Spirit. A good prayer meeting is like a symphony with the Holy Spirit as the conductor. If all the participants are listening to the Spirit, it will be as beautiful as a symphony with synergy, unique voices, unity, different levels of volume, a variety of tools used, no microphone hogs, and delightful surprises.

I have been in prayer meetings where we were told to only pray one type of prayer. This takes the baton out of the Holy Spirit's hand and puts it in the hands of a controlling or religious spirit. A controlling spirit controls, and a religious spirit says "this is the way we always do it; we are to follow the rules, not the Spirit." A leader can definitely set the tone for a prayer meeting. For example, they may say, "We want to repent over the sins in our city," or, "We really want to intercede for Stan," or, "We want to hear from the Lord and exercise our authority with proclamations." All this is great and part of the responsibility of the leader, but we as leaders need to remember the baton is in the Holy Spirit's hand, and we want Him leading the orchestration.

We often think the key to getting our prayers answered is to pray hard. Effort is important, but knowing where to make the effort is even more important. "Okay," you say, "but how do I know which type of prayer to pray?" We must listen to the Holy Spirit. We also need to know the different types of prayer, so we know when and how to use each tool. Praying in a group can help us grow in prayer. Most people pray like the people they regularly pray with, so broaden your exposure by praying with different groups. Again, the key is to learn to use all the types of prayer and then yield to the Holy Spirit.

Let's look at seven types of prayers. They are not in order, like a progression you need to move through, but put in an acrostic so that you can recall them if needed. A-P-R-I-E-S-T. A priest. "But you are a chosen people, a royal priesthood, a holy nation, God's special possession, that you may declare the praises of him who called you out of darkness into his wonderful light" (1 Peter 2:9). I like the way The Passion Translation calls the royal priesthood "**priests who are kings**."

If we can genuinely grab ahold of the truth that we are priests who are kings in Christ, it will enable us to wield these seven types of prayers in ways that influence those around us, change cities, and impact nations. Priests know how to minister to God and others, and kings know how to rule and reign. Praying believers need to know how to do both.

A-Adoration

P-Proclamation

R-Repentance

I-Intercessory

E-Emotional Sighs

S-Silence

T-Thanksgiving

Adoration

When we adore or exalt someone or something, we make it big in our eyes. "O magnify the Lord with me, And let us exalt His name together!" (Psalm 34:3 NKJV). When we spend time adoring Him, we enthrone Him in our hearts, home, or city. We express love and honor. We see His greatness and power. We are reminded of His faithfulness and mercy. As I said in an earlier chapter, it is helpful to make a list of His attributes in the back of our Bibles to help us flow in this type of prayer. This way, if we need to prime the pump in our prayers of adoration, we can turn there and start, "You, oh God, are magnificent. You are glorious. You are powerful and great, faithful and kind." After a time spent adoring Him, He seems larger and our problems seem smaller. It also positions us in a place of trust and gratefulness.

Proclamation

Cindy Jacobs explains in her excellent book *The Power of Persistent Prayer,* "Proclamation prayer is decreeing the will of God done on earth as it is in heaven. It brings God's will to earth, as it is in heaven. The Lord's Prayer is a type of this prayer (Matthew 6:9–13). It can yield dramatic results!"[1] She added, "Proclamation prayers are a form of intercession where God's will is decreed over a situation and anything contrary is brought into alignment."[2]

She goes on to describe the tools of Proclamation Prayer (emphasis added):

1. Binding and loosing—This prayer will bind the work of the enemy and loose the legal will of God into a given situation. *(Just a reminder the enemy works in unlawful or illegal ways, while the Lord's ways are legal and permitted.)*

2. Scripture proclamation—Choosing appropriate Scripture passages *(she implies, but I will state, just for clarity, this is under the leading of the Holy Spirit)* to proclaim the will of God.

3. Decrees—Speaking a prophetic word from God in order to change a current situation that is contrary to the will of God.

4. Declarations—Declaring the will of God under the inspiration and guidance of the Holy Spirit.[3]

Most of us have been taught prayer is one thing: *asking.* "God, would you save him?" "God, please heal her." "God, we really need rent money." "God, please bless her." Prayers like this are normal for us. Often, these types of prayers are called priestly prayers because we are serving as a priest standing between God and man. But as Cindy points out, Jesus responded to the disciples' request for instruction on how to pray with what we call The Lord's Prayer, which is full of proclamations.

"Thy Kingdom come. Thy will be done on earth, as it is in heaven" (Matthew 6:10, KJV).

Although Jesus Himself taught us to pray the Lord's Prayer using decrees and declarations, these declarations will not be effective if we declare from a place of our own will that hasn't been submitted to the Lord. Many love to quote Job 22:28 (NASB) which states, "You will also decree a thing, and it will be established for you; And light will shine on your ways." This is the truth, and we can build our prayer life on this, but we sometimes forget the verses that precede verse 28.

"Please receive instruction from His mouth and establish His words in your heart. If you return to the Almighty, you will be restored; If you remove unrighteousness far from your tent, and place your gold in the dust, and the gold of Ophir among the stones of the brooks, Then the Almighty will be your gold and choice silver to you. For then you will delight in the Almighty and lift up your face to God. You will pray to Him, and He will hear you and you will pay your vows" (Job 22:22–27 NASB).

There is a great deal of surrender in those six verses!

- Receive instruction from the Lord.
- Establish the Word in your heart.
- Return to the Lord and be restored
- Lay down all things of value to you (your gold and silver).
- Make the Lord your treasure.
- Delight in the Lord.
- Spend time with Him, face to face.

- Pray to Him.
- Pay your vows.

Then you will decree a thing and it will be established for you.

One of the first times in Scripture where we see God telling someone to exercise their authority was when Moses was leading the people out of captivity. "Then the LORD said to Moses, 'Why are you crying out to me? Tell the Israelites to move on. Raise your staff and stretch out your hand over the sea to divide the water so that the Israelites can go through the sea on dry ground. I will harden the hearts of the Egyptians so that they will go in after them'" (Exodus. 14:15–17).

He might say to us today, "Why are you praying to me? I have given you authority. Lead those who are following you to step out in faith. Speak to what is holding you back and blocking your way and tell it to part so that you can move forward."

There are times when Jesus prayed what we would call a typical "asking" prayer, as in John 17, but most of the time, He would command, decree, and declare. One interesting time was early in the morning when Jesus was going back to the city with His disciples. He saw a fig tree and went to it to get some figs, but it was without figs, so He declared, "May you never bear fruit again!" Matthew continues in Matthew 21:19 to explain it withered immediately. The disciples marveled at how quickly it withered. "Jesus replied, 'Listen to the truth. If you do not doubt God's power and speak out of faith's fullness, you can also speak to a tree, and it will wither away. Even more than that, you could say to this mountain, 'Be lifted up and be thrown into the sea' and it will be done. Everything you pray for with the fullness of faith you will receive!'" (Matthew. 21:21–22, TPT) Observe how Jesus made a proclamation and then in the next verse called it a prayer. Jesus seems to have a broader definition of prayer than many of us do. Notice he said to not doubt God's power but speak with faith's fullness. Recognizing what type of prayer or action He desires can be a challenge, but it helps us pray more effectively.

Many have tried to understand why Jesus cursed the fig tree. In fact, if you google "Why did Jesus curse the fig tree?" you will have over a million hits. I don't want to be simplistic, but a teacher teaches and uses every opportunity they can to teach. It is important to realize that many of our experiences in life are to teach us about our authority. We practice on small things, grow our faith, and then have faith for the next mountain that needs to go into the sea. The Lord loves to plant faith in His people. No matter what type of prayer we pray, we need to combine our prayer with faith. I had been a believer for less than a year when the Lord gave me an experience that caused my faith to grow.

I loved to play basketball. Blessed with height and excellent coaches who taught me the fundamentals of the game, I worked hard to become good enough to play in college. During this season of my life, I started dating Jack, a thrower on the track and field team.

Our team looked forward to a busy weekend. Thursday we played at home, then after the game my teammates and I loaded up and drove most of the night for a game on Friday night, and traveled again to a game on Saturday night. Prior to the game on Thursday, I removed a necklace that Jack had given me. It was a single pearl on a simple gold chain. Simple, elegant, and full of meaning to me. I always did one of three things with that necklace. (I know for some of you the idea that I wouldn't do the same thing every time is strange. I agree, but it is me and it is why I always must find my purse before I leave the house, even to this day!) I would hang it from the hook in the locker, put it in my pants pocket, or put it in my coat pocket.

We won the game that night and quickly loaded onto the bus for the long drive. As soon as I was settled on the bus, I realized that I hadn't put on my necklace. I reached into my pants pockets and didn't find it there. "That's funny, I thought I put it in my pants pocket." Next, I checked both of my coat pockets. *Right pocket, empty. Left pocket, empty.* Not just no necklace, but completely empty. Next, I went back to my pants pockets to check more thoroughly. Nothing. "*Oh well*" I thought, "*I must have hung it up in the locker.*" All weekend as I would put on my coat, I felt in my pockets for the treasured necklace.

As we pulled back into the gym after a long weekend, I could think of nothing else but going to the locker and checking to see if my necklace was still hanging on the hook in the locker. The metal hook was empty. I emptied the locker to make sure it hadn't fallen to the bottom of the locker. I also scanned the floor all around the locker. Again, nothing. Discouraged, disappointed and tired, I went home.

Before practice on Monday, I went early to talk with the janitor who cleaned the locker room to see if she had found the necklace. Again, nothing. During practice, I focused on practice and tried not to think about the necklace. I knew Jack would be kind about it, but I was very disappointed.

After practice, I gathered my stuff, and I headed out to the car. As I walked down the long hall, I breathed a silent prayer. "Lord, I don't need that necklace. All I need is You, but I sure would love to have that necklace back." As the February wind hit my face, I put my hands in my coat pocket to protect them against the cold. Immediately I felt it, the necklace! What a seed of faith was planted in my spirit on that frigid February day!

Repentance

"Repent, then, and turn to God, so that your sins may be wiped out, that times of refreshing may come from the Lord" (Acts 3:19). In the New Testament, repentance is frequently translated from the Greek word *metanoeo*. It means to "change the mind, relent, or change one's mind or disposition toward God."[4]

Again, the Holy Spirit is key in this type of prayer. He keeps us out of condemnation (see Romans. 8:1) and instead, walks us through conviction and into forgiveness. There is a marked difference between conviction and condemnation. The Lord convicts us of our specific sin and wants to restore close fellowship in our relationship with Him. On the other hand, condemnation is sent by the enemy and brings with it a general feeling of unworthiness and failure. Condemnation makes us want to hide from God and stay in discouragement. We can get in a place of religious repentance, where we are never clean enough to come to the Lord. We don't understand the finished work of the cross, and we go into a place of morbid introspection. The Holy Spirit knows what has been forgiven and what attitudes and behaviors we still need to repent for. We can trust Him to guide us. If we use our own mind to guide our repentance, we may ask forgiveness for acts already forgiven and ignore our hidden pet sins. These cherished sins are the sins we are so comfortable with that we no longer see them as sin. For some it might be gossip, for some it could be premarital sex, it might be miserliness hidden behind a facade of frugality, or perhaps worry. This is why it is key to listen to the Holy Spirit when we are repenting.

The other side of this coin of repentance is a casualness to our sin. I wonder if we appear to God like a three year old who yells "Sorry" over their shoulder as they run off to play again and get into more trouble. No real repentance, just going through a ritual. We need the fear of the Lord. A deep awe of who He is and genuine desire to please Him and be in close relationship with Him.

It is important that our hearts are clean as we approach the throne as believers:

> Who, then, ascends into the presence of the Lord? And who has the privilege of entering into God's Holy Place? Those who are clean—whose works and ways are pure, whose

hearts are true and sealed by the truth, those who never deceive, whose words are sure (Psalm 24:3–4, TPT).

Just like cars have unique blind spots, so do people. Therefore, David prayed, "Search me, God, and know my heart; test me and know my anxious thoughts. See if there is any offensive way in me, and lead me in the way everlasting" (Psalm 139:23–24).

David knew that sinful or offensive ways and worry or anxious thoughts are open doors the enemy uses to harass us. Keeping these doors shut is vital to joy and freedom. Part of the prayer of repentance is silence. We can't hear the Holy Spirit convict us unless we have learned to be still in His presence. If we respond to His conviction, there is great comfort in the following verse: "But if we freely admit our sins when his light uncovers them, he will be faithful to forgive us every time. God is just to forgive us our sins because of Christ, and he will continue to cleanse us from all unrighteousness" (1 John 1:9 TPT).

Intercession

Intercession is the most common type of prayer. This is a priestly prayer offered on behalf of ourselves or someone else. Most prayer meetings consist primarily of this type of prayer. These prayers cover a broad spectrum, such as a generic blessing, a request for physical healing, a specific prayer for $200 for the rest of someone's rent money, or the salvation of a friend. This is how most of us learned to pray. We learned that God answered prayer and grew in our faith concerning God's desire to answer prayer.

My prayer life received a huge boost when I learned to ask the Lord how to pray in specific situations. He tells us in John 10:27 (CEV), "His sheep know His voice." We can ask how to pray, we can hear His desire, and then we can pray in accordance with His will. We call this prophetic intercession.

Prayer is a dialogue. In contrast, many of us have a prayer life that resembles a monologue. The dialogue can be God's Word speaking to us and us responding by praying His Word back to Him. We might say, "Your Word says . . ." Other times we might insert a loved one's name into the Scripture. In addition, the dialogue might be asking questions and then waiting patiently for the answer. My friend and mentor Jean Steffenson says, "So much of effective prayer is asking good questions." She tells the story of when she started asking the Lord questions.

"I would ask the Lord a question and then sit and wait for the answer. I wasn't going to get up until I heard an answer. I was determined to wait. I told the Lord I wasn't moving until I heard from Him. At first it seemed to take a long time, but later it seemed the answers came more quickly. Maybe He knew I was serious about hearing from Him. You must expect Him to answer your question, or how do you have faith He will answer your prayers?"

I have learned much from her questions. Here are some questions I ask now:

- What is your heart in this situation?
- Where are you working, God?
- Where is the devil working?
- What do I need the most?
- What am I seeing in this situation?
- What am I not seeing in this situation?
- What do I need to believe you for?
- What is ruling in this region?

In the beginning, she encouraged us to ask yes or no questions to help us be able to hear.

Many times, we start in this position of priestly prayer as we make intercession. After hearing what God desires in the situation, we might pivot from asking the Lord to do something into our kingly role. From there we can exercise the authority He has given us as we partner with Him and proclaim what He desires. (see Proclamation Prayer above).

Emotional Sighs

"And in a similar way, the Holy Spirit takes hold of us in our human frailty to empower us in our weakness. For example, at times we don't even know how to pray, or know the best things to ask for. But the Holy Spirit rises up within us to super-intercede on our behalf, pleading to God with emotional sighs too deep for words" (Romans 8:26 TPT).

We can fall into the trap of believing the eloquence of our prayers is what captures the heart of the Father and gets our prayers answered. Even though the prayer of the Pharisee in Mark 8:9-14 was eloquent, God was not pleased with it. God is looking for genuine honesty. Sometimes when we are in a place of genuine honesty, we can't even form words. All we can do is cry and sigh. There are times, according to Romans 8:26, when the Holy Spirit takes those sighs to the Father. Often, we don't see our sighs as prayers, but any sound or look directed toward God, He receives.

At times, the sighs originate with us, and the Holy Spirit interprets them. In contrast, I have also seen the Lord use us as conduits of what He is feeling. One day the Lord led me to confront a leader who I worked closely with. The leader rejected what I shared. I immediately started weeping. Not just a few quiet tears, but an embarrassing, ugly cry. The strange thing was, I didn't feel mad or sad or rejected, or any other emotion. I knew I was crying for the Holy Spirit. It was as if the Holy Spirit was grieving through me. All this fits under the umbrella of emotional sighs.

Silence

How is silence part of prayer? Have you ever been around someone who was so wound up, they couldn't stop talking? Many of us are in that same state as we begin to pray with all our words gushing out. Listening is a vital part of prayer. We can't listen if words are pouring out of our mouths or flying around in our minds. Learning to be silent is a vital part of prayer. Being in a place of peace helps us as we listen to the Lord. A conversation occurs when there is a give and take, and each person shares and listens. Our Lord desires to have a conversation with us.

"Surrender your anxiety! Be still and stop and realize that I am God" (Psalm 46:10a TPT). "Let your heart be always guided by the peace of the Anointed One, who called you to peace as part of His one body. And always be thankful" (Colossians 3:15 TPT).

Thanksgiving

We give thanks to the Lord because He deserves it and is worthy. We want to be like the one leper who, out of the ten, chose to give thanks after Jesus healed him (see Luke 17:11–19). Too often, we gladly receive blessings from the Lord, but we forget to show gratitude. Gratefulness may not be our default setting, but we can grow in this area. Just like listening to testimonies of the Lord's great work, taking the time to give thanks bears similar good fruit. It helps us grow in our faith.

Psalm 107:22 (NKJV) encourages us, "Let them sacrifice the sacrifices of thanksgiving, And declare His works with rejoicing."

I have a friend who has the gift of healing and is a trained doctor. One time, during a time of worship, she had a vision of a room in heaven with all types of body parts. She felt the Lord was giving her access in prayer for creative miracles to be performed where people would receive healing with new body parts. She asked, "How do we bring them to earth?" The Lord answered, "With thanksgiving."

"Be saturated in prayer throughout each day, offering your faith-filled requests before God with overflowing gratitude" (Philippians 4:6 TPT). We are also encouraged to "Enter his gates with thanksgiving and his courts with praise. Give thanks to him and praise his name" (Psalm 100:4).

"He who offers a sacrifice of thanksgiving honors Me" (Psalm 50:23 NASB).

What are we missing out on in our prayer life because we are forgetting to be thankful?

When we have all these prayer tools in our tool chest, and we yield to the Spirit, hearing His voice, realizing we are priests who are kings, then we are positioned to pray effectively. We interact with the Lord, overcome the enemy, and see His kingdom come and His will be done.

Father God,

I desire to pray as a priest who is a king. First help me to always remember to minister to You first. Grant me wisdom and revelation. Guide me as I partner with You. Teach me to operate in each of these types of prayer so that it becomes a natural part of my prayer life. Help me to listen to the Holy Spirit so the most effective type of prayer can be used and your kingdom will be expanded. In Jesus' Name, Amen.

Conclusion

It has been an honor to be on this journey with you as we have worked on troubleshooting your prayer life. I pray your discouragement has lifted, your hope has been restored, and your foundation strengthened. Please remember, prayer is more than accomplishing something in the kingdom. It is about building a relationship with a God who loves you deeply. All we do flows from our relationship with Him. Are you ready to boldly step out with Jesus in praying faith-filled prayers? We only lose if we quit! You will need perseverance, but God will give you the strength you need. When God created you, He had good works for you to do: "We have become his poetry, a re-created people that will fulfill the destiny he has given each of us, for we are joined to Jesus, the Anointed One. Even before we were born, God planned in advance *our destiny* and the good work we would do *to fulfill it!*" (Ephesians 2:10 TPT) I trust this book has helped you get back on course so you grow in your relationship with Him and can accomplish all the Father desires. I hope what I've learned on my journey will make your journey more peaceful and productive.

References

Prayer

1. Dr. Harold Eberle, *Systematic Theology for the New Apostolic Reformation* (Yakima, WA: Worldcast Publishing, 2015), p. 819.

Chapter 2

1. Ira Levin, Stepford Wives (New York: William Morrow Paperbacks, 2004).

2. Dallas Willard, Hearing God (Downers Grove, IL: InterVarsity Press, 1999).

Chapter 4

1. Jay Livingston and Ray Evans, "Que Sera, Sera," Columbia Records, 1956.

Chapter 5

1. Quin Sherrer and Ruthanne Garlock, How to Pray for Your Children (Ventura, CA: Regal Books, 1998).

Chapter 6

1. Joyce Meyer, "Notes and Commentary," in The Everyday Life Bible (New York: Faith Words, 2009).

Chapter 8

1. Spiros Zodhiates, ed., Hebrew-Greek Keyword Study Bible (Chattanooga, TN: AMG Publishers, 1996), p. 1603.

2. Dutch Sheets, Authority in Prayer: Praying with Power and Purposes (Bethany, MN: Bethany House, 2015).

Chapter 10

1. Dutch Sheets, Power of Hope (Lake Mary, FL: Charisma House, 2014), p. 8.

2. Dutch Sheets, Tell Your Heart to Beat Again (Ventura, CA: Regal Books, 2002), p. 25.

3. Dutch Sheets, Power of Hope (Lake Mary, FL: Charisma House, 2014), p. 17-18.

4. Dutch Sheets, Tell Your Heart to Beat Again (Ventura, CA: Regal Books, 2002), p. 37.

Chapter 12

1. Dana Candler, First Love (Ada, MI: Chosen Books, 2022), p. 78-79.

Chapter 14

1. "Strong's H5749," Blue Letter Bible, https://www.blueletterbible.org/lexicon/h5749/kjv/wlc/0-1/.

2. Jack Hayford, ed., Word Wealth, NKJV Spirit Filled Life Bible, 3rd Edition (Nashville, TN: Thomas Nelson, 2018), p. 1534.

Chapter 15

1. Kelly's Heroes, directed by Brian G. Hutton (1970; Katzka-Loeb Productions), DVD.

2. Dana Candler, First Love (Ada, MI: Chosen Books, 2022), p. 78-79.

Chapter 16

1. https://www.youtube.com/watch?v=SigF6cYSZcw

Chapter 17

1. "Mundane," Dictionary.com, https://www.dictionary.com/browse/mundane.

2. "Banal," Dictionary.com, https://www.dictionary.com/browse/banal.

3. Sheldon Vanauken, Severe Mercy (San Francisco, CA: Harper One, 2009).

Chapter 18

1. Dutch Sheets, Intercessory Prayer (Ventura, CA: Regal Books, 1996), p. 16.

2. Ibid., p. 17.

Chapter 19

1. "Strong's G154," Blue Letter Bible, https://www.blueletterbible.org/lexicon/g154/kjv/tr/0-1/.

2. Text Source: "Book Review: EntreLeadership by Dave Ramsey," MicroCapClub, http://microcapclub.com/2012/03/book-review-entreleadership-by-dave-ramsey/, inspired by Dave Ramsey, EntreLeadership (Brentwood, TN: Howard Books, 2011).

Chapter 20

1. "Goodreads Quotes, Corrie ten Boom," https://www.goodreads.com/quotes/692322-we-never-know-how-god-will-answer-our-prayers-but.

2. Arthur Wallis, Rain From Heaven (London: Hodder & Stoughton, 1979), p. 106.

3. Nicky van der Drift, "Sophie Scholl—White Rose Resistance," International Bomb Command Centre, April 30, 2020, https://internationalbcc.co.uk/aboutibcc/news/sophiescholl/#:~:text=%E2%80%9CHow%20can%20we%20expect%20righteousness,awakened%20and%20stirred%20to%20action%3F%E2%80%9D.

Chapter 23

1. "Presumption," Webster's Dictionary 1828, https://webstersdictionary1828.com/Dictionary/presumption.

2. "Presume," Dictionary.com, https://dictionary.com/browse/presume.

3. Gwen Osborne and Barbara Parks, This End Up: Structure for the Organic Church (Texarkana, TX: Phao Books, 2013), p. 115.

4. Agnes Sanford, The Healing Light (New York: Ballantine Books, 1983), p. 19.

5. Ibid, p. 159-60

Chapter 24

1. Jim Folk, "Anxiety Disorder Statistics and Facts," Anxiety Centre, November 20, 2021, https://www.anxietycentre.com/statistics/anxiety-disorder-statistics-facts/.

2. Corrie ten Boom, "Quote," Quotefancy, https://quotefancy.com/quote/789784/Corrie-ten-Boom-Worrying-is-carrying-tomorrow-s-load-with-today-s-strength-carrying-two.

Chapter 26

1. Spiros Zodhiates, Th.D., ed., Hebrew-Greek Keyword Study Bible (Chattanooga, TN: AMG Publishers, 1996), p. 1601, New Testament word 1182.

2. "Strongs NT 1097," Thayer's Greek Lexicon, Bible Hub, https://biblehub.com/thayers/1097.htm.

3. Henri J. M. Nouwen, Life of the Beloved (Hachette, UK, Crossroad, 2002).

4. Jack Frost, Spiritual Slavery to Spiritual Sonship: Your Destiny Awaits You (Shippensburg, PA: Destiny Image Publishers, 2013).

Chapter 27

1. Brian Simmons, The Passion Translation (Savage, MN: BroadStreet Publishing, 2020), p. 112.

2. Ibid., p. 112.

3. Stephen Crosby, Authority, Accountability and the Apostolic Movement (Enumclaw, WA: Pleasant Word, 2006), p. xxv-xxvi.

4. Brene Brown, Daring Greatly: How the Courage to be Vulnerable Transforms the Way We Live, Love, Parent and Lead (New York: Avery, 2015), p. 1.

Chapter 28

1. Cindy Jacobs, The Power of Persistent Prayer (Ada, MI: Bethany House, 2010), p. 140.

2. Ibid, p. 143.

3. Ibid, p. 155-156

4. Spiros Zodhiates, Th.D., ed., Hebrew-Greek Keyword Study Bible (Chattanooga, TN: AMG Publishers, 1996), p. 1651, New Testament word 3556.